SESSIONS OF THE PEACE
FOR BEDFORDSHIRE
1355–1359, 1363–1364

Edited by
ELISABETH G. KIMBALL

HISTORICAL MANUSCRIPTS COMMISSION
JP16

SESSIONS OF THE PEACE
FOR BEDFORDSHIRE

1355-1359, 1363-1364

Edited by

ELISABETH G. KIMBALL

LONDON
HER MAJESTY'S STATIONERY OFFICE
1969

This volume, which has been prepared by the Bedfordshire Historical Record Society, forms No. 48 in the series issued by that Society and No. 16 in the *Joint Publication* series published by Her Majesty's Stationery Office for the Historical Manuscripts Commission.

Printed in England for Her Majesty's Stationery Office, by J. W. Arrowsmith Ltd., Winterstoke Road, Bristol BS3 2NT.

SBN 11 440008 3*

CONTENTS

PREFACE

The publication in this volume of two rolls of the Bedfordshire justices of the peace by the Bedfordshire Historical Record Society marks the completion of a task begun by the late Bertha H. Putnam. With the exception of a roll for Buckinghamshire too illegible to be transcribed, all the records of justices of the peace for counties discovered by Miss Putnam are now in print in full or by excerpt. Although Miss Putnam published selected cases from the earlier and longer of the Bedfordshire rolls in *Proceedings before the Justices of the Peace in the Fourteenth and Fifteenth Centuries* (London, 1938) and used material from the second roll in her discussion of the work of the justices in this same volume, the decision of the Bedfordshire Historical Record Society to print the two rolls in full is a happy one. As will appear, each provides information on the work of the justices which supports that provided in the records for other counties already in print. Also by this means the corpus of available peace rolls is augmented.

To the officials of the Public Record Office, both those in the Round Room and those who appear when needed, I can never adequately express my thanks. I wish also to acknowledge the assistance of the staff of the Firestone Library of Princeton University. My dependence on Miss Putnam's work on the justices of the peace is apparent throughout.

E.G.K.

LIST OF ABBREVIATIONS

Bassett, *Knights of the Shire*	Bassett, Margery, *Knights of the Shire for Bedfordshire during the Middle Ages* (Bedfordshire Historical Record Society, xxix, Streatley, 1949).
C.C.R.	*Calendar of Close Rolls.*
C.F.R.	*Calendar of Fine Rolls.*
C.P.R.	*Calendar of Patent Rolls.*
G.D.R.	Gaol Delivery Roll.
K.B.	King's Bench Roll.
List of Sheriffs	Public Record Office, Lists and Indexes, ix, *List of Sheriffs for England and Wales* (London, 1898).
Members of Parliament	*Returns of Members of Parliament, Accounts and Papers*, xvii, part i (1878), *Parliaments of England, 1213–1702.*
List of Escheators	Public Record Office, List of Escheators.
Putnam, *Proceedings*	*Proceedings before the Justices of the Peace in the Fourteenth and Fifteenth Centuries*, ed. by B. H. Putnam (The Ames Foundation, London, 1938).

INTRODUCTION

GENERAL BACKGROUND

The middle years of the fourteenth century, the years covered by the extant records of the Bedfordshire justices of the peace, were years of great activity and, to the historian of medieval England, they are years of great interest. The Treaty of Calais (1361) marked the end of a phase of the Hundred Years' War during which the English had won the battles of Crecy and Sluys. Edward III was at the height of his powers, having not yet relaxed to others the control of the kingdom. The Black Death and the social and economic discontent which produced, on the one hand, the Statute of Labourers of 1351 and, on the other, the Peasants' Revolt of 1381 were helping to change the face of rural England. John Wyclif with his radical religious ideas was about to make his appearance. But interesting and important as these developments were, this is not the place to discuss them. The Bedfordshire peace rolls contain no specific references to the effect of the French war or to the Black Death, nor is it apparent that the crimes recorded on these rolls were the result of special circumstances existing in the county or in the country. This absence of timeliness is not surprising. The rolls are the records of a single county for a brief period. During the years covered by the earlier roll, c. 1355–1359, violations of the Statute of Labourers were handled by especially appointed justices of labourers, so that offences of an economic nature did not come before the justices of the peace as they did after the justices of labourers were discontinued in 1359. But probably more important is the fact that the justices of the peace were concerned with everyday law enforcement, with the type of offence which was committed whatever conditions at home or abroad. Undoubtedly the whole country was affected by the events mentioned above, but there was no occasion for juries reporting local crimes or trying those accused of such crimes to speculate about the causes or to comment on general conditions. Thus these rolls will provide the historian with a picture of crime in Bedfordshire which must be studied in relation to what was happening elsewhere in England during the same years, the genealogist with the names of many local inhabitants, and the student of the history of judicial procedure with some details on how the justices of the peace conducted their business.[1] For a picture of how rural England

---

[1] For a general discussion see Putnam, *Proceedings*, introduction, *passim*.

was affected by the events of the mid-fourteenth century one must look elsewhere.

THE BEDFORDSHIRE PEACE ROLLS

The two peace rolls for Bedfordshire printed in this volume are in the Public Record Office (Just. Itin. 1/32 and 33). They pertain to the middle of the fourteenth century, one to the years *c.* 1355–1359, the other to 1363–1364. Both rolls are in good condition and both show evidence of careful and systematic preparation. For ease of reference they have been designated Roll A and Roll B.

Roll A consists of seven membranes written on both sides.[1] It cannot be dated exactly because the indictments are not enrolled under session headings and so it is not known on what dates sessions were held. The Bedfordshire peace commission of 20 January 1355 is enrolled on the first membrane; the latest offence, which is not the last one enrolled, was committed on 28 August 1359.[2] Presumably the first session for which business is recorded on the roll was held soon after the receipt of the commission, in the early months of 1355, and the latest session in the autumn or early winter of 1359. Thus the roll probably covers approximately five years. Because there are no session headings there is no information about where the sessions were held or what justices were present, except as references to sessions of the peace appear elsewhere. The roll contains 177 entries and some sixty jury lists. On the evidence of the places named in the cases it seems likely that the juries represented hundreds and the town of Bedford, not larger or smaller sections of the county. Fines made by trespassers and the names of pledges were recorded for those who had admitted guilt. Outlawry for failure to appear for trial and acquittals were also recorded as was the fact that an offender had been before the King's Bench or been tried by the justices of gaol delivery. The amount of fines and the fact of other process were noted in the margin. Two writs of *cerciorari* and two of *mandamus* were enrolled. One of the former dated 12 November 1357 summoned the last five indictments on m. 7d. before the King's Bench.[3] The name Derby at the end of the roll may be that of the clerk.

Roll B which consists of four membranes written on both sides is a very different document from the earlier roll. It records, under session headings, the business done at eight sessions of the peace held in Bedfordshire from 14 March 1363 through 8 January 1364. It also contains a copy of the Bedfordshire peace commission of 20 November 1362 under which the sessions were held. As presently arranged the membranes do

---

[1] Selected cases from this roll are printed in Putnam, *Proceedings*, pp. 43–61.
[2] See below p. 93, no. 166.
[3] Below p. 98.

not seem to be in the order intended. Mm. 4 and 4d. which contain the commission and some of the records of the 14 March 1363 session should probably begin the roll. Then mm. 3, 3d., 2, 2d., 1d., and 1 should follow in that order. For ease in tracing procedure which for many offenders is continued for more than one session, the membranes have been printed in the order indicated above. Dates for all sessions and frequently the place of the sitting and the justices present were given. The presenting juries were not named.

The roll though brief is most interesting. It appears to be not a record of all business done at these eight sessions but rather the record of the business which the justices had completed prior to and at their latest recorded session, 8 January 1364. The results of trials were noted, as were summons for trial and reports of the outlawry of those who failed to appear. A separate roll of fines, no longer extant, was kept, so the amounts of the fines and the names of pledges do not appear on the peace roll.

Why these two rolls were prepared and how they came to be preserved are questions for which there are no ready answers. Miss Putnam showed that many peace rolls, particularly those for the later years of the reign of Edward III and for that of Richard II, are extant because of visits made by the King's Bench to the county concerned. During such visits lesser jurisdictions were suspended and their unfinished business handled by the justices of the King's Bench. Undetermined indictments were, therefore, enrolled for the convenience of the Bench. When the Bench returned to Westminster it took with it the peace rolls as well as its own records.[4]

This explanation will not account for the preparation or the preservation of the two Bedfordshire peace rolls which record chiefly determined indictments or the outlawry of offenders who failed to appear before the justices of the peace for trial. Although the King's Bench did visit Bedfordshire in Michelmas term 1357, during the period covered by the cases on Roll A, there is evidence that the roll could not have been prepared for this visit.[5] When in Bedfordshire the Bench sat at Dunstable and while there delivered Bedford gaol. The presiding judge, Notton, sent a writ to Lord Grey, justice of the peace for Bedfordshire and probably *capitalis iusticiarius*, asking that indictments undetermined by the justices of the peace be sent to him without delay. This writ, the last entry on the peace roll, was noted by the clerk to apply to five indictments which are enrolled on m. 7d. just before the writ.[6] He did send the indictments to the Bench and the offenders were not summoned for trial before

---

[4] Putnam, *Proceedings*, pp. lxiv ff.
[5] *Ibid.*, p. 31. Michelmas 31 Edward III. Miss Putnam suggests that Roll A was before the Bench on the writ of *cerciorari; ibid.*, p. 58.
[6] Below pp. 95–98, nos. 172–177.

the justices of the peace. They did not, however, appear before the Bench while it was in Dunstable but in 1358 two of them made fines before the Bench at Westminster.[7] The clerk, nevertheless, kept the record of the indictments putting them at the end of the roll. Whether sessions of the peace were suspended during the visit of the Bench to Bedfordshire cannot be determined because of the absence of session headings on the roll. Inasmuch as a substantial number of the offences on the roll were committed after Michelmas 1357, it can be assumed that if the Bedfordshire justices of the peace did not sit during that term, they resumed their sessions on the departure of the Bench. Furthermore, the whole roll did not go before the Bench because the clerk enrolled business which, in view of the dates of the offences involved, must have been done in 1358 and 1359. Although the date of the session at which a presentment was made cannot be fixed by the date of the offence, except for the cases sent to the Bench for trial which are enrolled on the dorse of m. 7, it does seem from the dates of the offences that the enrolment probably represents fairly well the order of the sessions. Since some of these must have postdated the visit of the Bench, the roll cannot have been prepared for that visit and cannot have been taken to Westminster with the records of the session at Dunstable. Additional support, if any is needed, for this conclusion is found in the fact that aside from the entries on m. 7d. the roll records chiefly business completed by the justices of the peace, business in which the Bench was not interested.

The compilation of Roll B which records only completed business presents a somewhat different problem.[8] The first two entries following the enrolment of the commission of 20 November 1362 have to do with an appeal that was not carried through and on which a writ of *cerciorari* was issued on 7 June 1364, five months after the date of the latest session recorded on the roll, 8 January 1364. The remainder of the business on the roll is concerned with fines made by trespassers, acquittals, and reports of outlawries of accused persons, both felons and trespassers, who failed to appear for trial. Some of the offenders had been indicted before the justices of the peace at the recorded sessions, some at previous essions. No visit of the King's Bench to Bedfordshire occurred during or soon after the dates of the sessions on this roll. It may be that the roll was sent to chancery in response to the writ of *cerciorari* on the appeal but if so this does not explain the enrolment of other business. Also chancery's record of the proceedings on the appeal, although probably prepared in response to the writ of *cerciorari*, may well have been copied from the peace roll.[9] Another possible explanation for the compilation of this

[7] Nos. 175, 176.

[8] Miss Putnam suggests this roll was before the Bench because of an appeal; Putnam, *Proceedings*, p. 34, n. 4; below pp. 102–104.

[9] Chancery Miscellany 47/5/125.

roll may relate to the new peace commissions issued for all counties in the spring of 1364. That for Bedfordshire included none of the three men who had been appointed in 1362.[10] The clerk may have drawn up Roll B to close out the completed business of the 1362 commission, although it would seem unlikely that the new justices were interested in the finished business of their predecessors.

There is, however, another and more plausible explanation for the enrolment and preservation of both rolls. A peace roll of 1361–1362 for the East Riding of Yorkshire contains a copy of a writ addressed to the presiding justice which cites a statute of 1335 and requests that before any rolls are delivered to the treasury, the estreats be sent to the exchequer.[11] Miss Putnam suggested that a similar writ, now lost, explained the preservation of another East Riding roll of the same date. The statute of 1335 provided for the annual delivery of records of justices of assize, gaol delivery, and oyer and terminer. While it did not originally cover the justices of the peace Miss Putnam thought it was in this writ extended to them.[12] If this was the case, it seems likely that writs similar to the East Riding writ, or at least a tacit understanding of the order the writ contained, operated in the case of the Bedfordshire justices of the peace. Certainly their rolls, like that of the East Riding, contain the record of finished business.[13] In Roll A the record of the amounts of the fines was incorporated into the body of the roll with the figures repeated in the margin, no doubt for the convenience of the exchequer officials. Thus the clerk probably intended the roll to serve both as a record of proceedings and as an estreat roll. In Roll B the amounts of the fines were not given but reference was made to a separate fine roll now lost. The omission from Roll B of the record of any unfinished business and the enrolment on m. 7d. of Roll A of a few unfinished cases rather as an afterthought would be accounted for by the purpose for which the rolls were compiled. Thus it is possible that both rolls were prepared, probably by different clerks because of their different form and because different justices were involved, for deposit at the treasury. Thus they were sent to Westminster and so preserved.

If, on the other hand, Roll B reached the treasury, the repository of legal records, by way of chancery, then Roll A somehow went with it. This latter happening seems unlikely since the same justices and probably

[10] C.P.R 1361–1364, p. 529.
[11] Yorkshire Sessions of the Peace, 1361–1364, ed. by B. H. Putnam (Yorkshire Archaeological Society, Record Series, C, Wakefield, 1939), p. 1; 9 Edward III, st. 1, c. 5; see also Putnam, Proceedings, pp. lxvi ff.
[12] Putnam, Yorkshire Sessions of the Peace, p. xix.
[13] For a 1340 peace roll for Cambridgeshire containing chiefly finished business the preservation of which cannot be accounted for by a visit of the King's Bench to Cambridgeshire, see Some Sessions of the Peace in Cambridgeshire in the Fourteenth Century, 1340, 1380–83, ed. by M. M. Taylor (Cambridge Antiquarian Society, Publications, LV, Cambridge, 1942), pp. xx–xxii.

the same clerk were not involved and since there are extant no records for the sessions of the peace known to have been held in the interval between those on the two rolls.[14] Rather, in view of the systematic character of the rolls, it seems probable that both and most certainly Roll A, were prepared because the justices were ordered, or thought they were ordered, like justices of other jurisdictions, to send their records to the treasury, if not annually at least periodically. Certainly there is in these rolls no evidence of the hasty compilation which is characteristic of many enrolments which were prepared because a visit of the King's Bench to the county was imminent.[15]

THE COMMISSIONS OF THE PEACE

The indictments enrolled on Roll A were heard by Bedfordshire justices acting under three commissions of the peace issued on 20 January 1355, 8 October 1355, and 20 May 1356. The sessions recorded on Roll B were heard under the peace commission of 20 November 1362.[1]

The first of these commissions, that of 20 January 1355, which is enrolled on m. 1 of Roll A, was addressed to nine men: Lord Grey of Ruthin, Sir Gerald de Braybrok, Sir Robert Thorpe, Hugh Sadelyngstanes, Geoffrey de Lucy, John Marshall of Wootton, Sir Peter de Salford, John de Rokesdon, and John de Arderne. The commission is of the type first issued in December 1352 when, because separate justices of labourers were commissioned, jurisdiction over the labour laws was omitted from the peace commission. The justices of the peace were charged with the enforcement of the two peace statutes, Winchester and Northampton, and with the supervision of array. They were also empowered to hear and determine felonies and trespasses. A quorum was named consisting of the two lawyers on the commission, one of whom was to be present when felons were tried.[2]

Although no notice of the fact is taken on the roll, two other peace commissions were issued for Bedfordshire during the period it covers, one on 8 October 1355 to Braybrok, Sir Thomas de Swyneford, Salford, and Rokesdon, and another on 20 May 1356 to Lord Grey, Braybrok, Swyneford, Thorpe, Sir John Knyvet, Marshall, and Rokesdon.[3] In form

[14] Pipe Roll 208, Beds, Noua Oblata; below p. 29.
[15] *Some Sessions of the Peace in Lincolnshire, 1381–1396*, I, ed. by E. G. Kimball (Lincoln Record Society, *Publications*, 49, Hereford, 1955), xi; Taylor, *Some Sessions of the Peace in Cambridgeshire*, pp. xxii–xxiii.
[1] On commissions of the peace see Putnam, *Proceedings*, pp. xix ff.; ' The Transformation of the Keepers of the Peace into Justices of the Peace, 1327–1380 ', Royal Historical Society, *Transactions*, 4th series, xii, 19–48 (London, 1929).
[2] *C.P.R.* 1354–1358, p. 122. This commission is printed below pp. 31–33 and in Putnam, *Proceedings*, pp. 43–44. On the quorum see *ibid.*, pp. xxv–xxvi.
[3] *C.P.R.* 1354–1358, pp. 226, 388.

these commissions are similar to that of 20 January 1355 except that no quorum was named. The presence of two lawyers, Thorpe and Knyvet, on the 1356 commission suggests that they were expected to serve in this capacity. The omission of sessions headings from the roll makes it impossible to tell which indictments were heard under which commission.

On 21 March 1361 a new peace commission was issued for Bedfordshire but no records of any of the sessions held under it have survived. The commission was addressed to Lord Grey, William de la Pole of Ashby, John Pygot, Salford, Thomas de Eston, and John FitzJohn.[4] On 20 November 1362 commissions of the peace were again issued to all counties. In this commission, addressed for Bedfordshire to Sir Thomas de Reynes, William de Riceby, and Eston, the justices were charged with the enforcement of the three peace statutes, Winchester, Northampton, and the Statute of Westminster of 1361. They were to hear and determine felonies and trespasses, including violations of the assize of weights and measures and of the labour laws, the justices of labourers having been discontinued in 1359. There was no quorum and the responsibility for array was withdrawn. Sessions were to be held four times a year within the dates specified in the statute of 1362: 9–13 January, the second week in Lent, Whitsunday–24 June, and 29 September–6 October.[5]

In personnel these five commissions showed considerable variation. The justices named in the 20 January 1355 and 20 May 1356 commissions were representative of the three groups from which justices of the peace were generally appointed in the fourteenth century.[6] There was a member of the local nobility, Lord Grey, and two justices of the central courts, Thorpe and Sadelyngstanes and Thorpe and Knyvet. The remaining members were gentry, chiefly local men, three of whom were named to both commissions. The commission of 21 March 1361, again headed by Lord Grey and composed otherwise of gentry had no lawyers on it. The two remaining commissions, 8 October 1355 and 20 March 1362, were composed only of gentry. On that of October 1355 there were four, three of whom had been on previous commissions; on the 1362 commission but three, only one of whom, Eston, had previously been named justice of the peace in Bedfordshire. Commissions of this later date for other counties were also small and composed only of gentry.[7] This fact

[4] *Ibid.*, 1361–1364, p. 64. This commission is printed in C. G. Crump and C. Johnson, ' The Powers of the Justices of the Peace ', *English Historical Review* (1912), xxvii 234–236; Putnam, *Yorkshire Sessions of the Peace*, pp. 1–3; *Rolls of the Gloucestershire Sessions of the Peace, 1361–1398*, ed. by E. G. Kimball (Bristol and Gloucestershire Archaeological Society, *Transactions*, 62, Kendal, 1942), pp. 58–61.

[5] *C.P.R.* 1361–1364, p. 292. This commission is printed below pp. 99–100 and in Putnam, *Yorkshire Sessions of the Peace*, pp. 42–44. 36 Edward III, st. 1, c. 12.

[6] Putnam, *Proceedings*, pp. lxxvi ff.

[7] *Ibid.*, p. lxxxii.

is surprising since the Statute of Westminster in 1361 had specified that commissions of the peace should include one magnate and some men learned in the law in addition to members of the gentry.[8]

THE JUSTICES OF THE PEACE

As has been said, the men appointed to the four mid-fourteenth-century peace commissions in Bedfordshire for which records of sessions are extant belonged to the three groups, peers, lawyers, and gentry, from which justices of the peace were commonly appointed in the middle ages.[1] It has also been pointed out that two of these commissions were composed only of gentry. As session headings are lacking for Roll A which contains indictments under the commissions of 20 January and 8 October 1355 and 20 May 1356, there is little evidence about which justices actually served. Evidence of service for the three members of the commission of 20 November 1362 is more extensive.

Magnates: Reynold or Reginald, second baron Grey of Ruthin (b. c. 1319; d. 1388), was the only peer appointed justice of the peace for Bedfordshire in the middle years of the fourteenth century. Although its title was taken from lands in Denbighshire, the Grey family's seat was at Wrest, Silsoe, in the parish of Flitton in Bedfordshire and they also held land at Great Brickhill in Buckinghamshire. On succeeding his father in 1353, Lord Grey was immediately appointed justice of the peace in Bedfordshire and frequently thereafter in both Bedfordshire and Buckinghamshire until his death in 1388. He was also named on commissions of array and of oyer and terminer in these counties and occasionally elsewhere. He served in the French war and in Wales. As has been noted Lord Grey was a member of the Bedfordshire peace commissions of 20 January 1355 and 20 May 1356 but not of the commission of 8 October 1355. He was again named justice of the peace on 21 March 1361 but not on 20 November 1362. He was, however, a member of the peace commissions of 1364 and 1368. It seems likely that he served actively as justice of the peace at least during much of the period covered by Roll A. Writs of *cerciorari* and *mandamus* ordering records sent to the King's Bench and to chancery addressed to Lord Grey and his associates were enrolled as having been addressed *michi*. A writ of 1362 instructing the justices on

---

[8] *Ibid.*, p. lxxix. Miss Putnam was unable to explain why the statute was ignored.

[1] See above p. 7. The biographies which follow are not intended to be complete; the information they contain shows the type of men appointed as justices of the peace. Justices appointed only to the commission of 21 March 1361 are not included.

the 21 March 1361 commission to turn over their unfinished business to their successors was directed to him and replies to all writs were made in his name. He was named on the pipe rolls as having accounted at the exchequer for the fines collected by the Bedfordshire justices of the peace in 1356–1358, 1359–1360, and 1361–1362, years when he was a member of the peace commission. More concrete evidence of his activity as justice of the peace is afforded by the report of an assault made on him in 1355 at Silsoe to prevent him from carrying out the duties of his office, an assault so violent that he nearly lost his life. In the report Lord Grey is called chief keeper of the peace and it was probably as *capitalis iusticiarius* that he performed the various functions mentioned above, although he was not so designated in the commission. That he was named first is of little significance as he was the only peer appointed. Lord Grey was also involved with the other side of the law. In 1352, before he had succeeded to the title, he was pardoned a fine of £20 in the King's Bench for trespasses and extortions in Bedfordshire. He was an ancestor of the Lord Grey who was involved in the notorious Bedford riot in 1439.[2]

Lawyers: Sir John Knyvet (d. 1381) of Northamptonshire was in 1357 a serjeant at law. In 1361 he was appointed justice of the Common Pleas, in 1365 chief justice of the King's Bench, and from 1372 to 1377 he served as chancellor. He was named to commissions of the peace, of labourers, and of oyer and terminer in Northamptonshire and various other counties, including the Bedfordshire peace commission of 20 May 1356. He served with Sir Robert Thorpe as justice of gaol delivery and was one of the justices who delivered Bedford and Dunstable gaols when felons indicted before the justices of the peace were tried. There is no evidence that he sat as justice of the peace for Bedfordshire although it was probably as a member of the quorum for the trial of felons that he was named to the commission of 20 May 1356.[3]

Hugh Sadelyngstanes, a member of the quorum of the Bedfordshire peace commission of 20 January 1355, had lands in Yorkshire and the eastern counties. He was pleading in the upper courts by 1355 but was not named to either bench. He was a member of numerous commissions of the peace and of oyer and terminer in the eastern counties in the 1340's and 1350's and in 1355 he served as justice of gaol delivery at Norwich,

---

[2] *The Complete Peerage*, i–xi, ed. by V. Gibbs (London, 1910–1949), *sub nomine;* Putnam, *Proceedings, sub nomine; C.P.R.; C.C.R.; C.F.R.; Select Cases before the King's Council, 1243–1482*, ed. by I. S. Leadam and J. F. Baldwin (Selden Society, xxxv, Cambridge, 1918), pp. cxi–cxiv; Pipe Roll 203, 205, 208, Beds, Noua Oblata; below pp. 32, 54, 59–60, 67, 96–98, 100–101, 104.

[3] Foss, E., *A Bibliographical Dictionary of the Judges of England, 1066–1870* (London, 1870), *sub nomine;* Putnam, *Proceedings*, p. 61; *C.P.R.; C.C.R.; C.F.R.;* G.D.R. 215/2, m. 224.

2

Dunstable, and in the north. As his name does not appear in the records after 1357 it may be presumed that he died in that year or shortly thereafter.[4]

Sir Robert Thorpe (d. 1372), a member of the quorum of the Bedfordshire peace commission of 20 January 1355 and probably of 20 May 1356, came from Thorpe next Norwich. Educated at Cambridge, he was for a time master of Pembroke College. He was pleading by 1340 and was a king's serjeant in 1345. In 1356 he was made chief justice of the Common Pleas and he succeeded William of Wykeham as chancellor in 1371. He was appointed to numerous commissions of the peace, as justice of labourers in Bedfordshire and elsewhere on the eastern circuit, and to many other commissions. As justice of gaol delivery he sometimes delivered Bedford and Dunstable gaols.[5]

Gentry: John de Arderne (d. 1375) was probably the son of Nicholas de Arderne of Buckinghamshire. He held lands in that country and in Bedfordshire and Warwickshire. He was appointed justice of the peace in Bedfordshire, Buckinghamshire, Hertfordshire, and Cambridgeshire, and on other commissions in those counties. He represented Buckinghamshire in parliament in 1362, 1366, and 1372 and was named sheriff of Bedfordshire and Buckinghamshire in 1374. He was a member of the Bedfordshire peace commission of 20 January 1355.[6]

Sir Gerald de Braybrok (d. 1359) held land in Cadbury (Eaton Socon), Clifton, Clophill and Cainhoe, Potton, and Blunham in Bedfordshire and land in neighbouring counties, which he inherited in 1324. He served on numerous commissions, chiefly in Bedfordshire and Buckinghamshire, being on the peace commission for Bedfordshire almost continually from 1344 until his death in 1359. He was also named to joint commissions of the peace and labourers in both counties and as justice of labourers in Bedfordshire. He was knight of the shire for Bedfordshire and Buckinghamshire sixteen times between 1332 and 1358. He served the two counties as sheriff in 1341 and 1352–1354 and as escheator in the latter years. His son Robert was bishop of London, 1382–1404, and chancellor, 1382–1383.[7]

[4] Putnam, *Proceedings*, p. 61; *C.P.R.; C.C.R.; C.F.R.;* Putnam, B. H., *The Place in Legal History of Sir William Shareshull* (*Cambridge Studies in English Legal History*, Cambridge, 1950), p. 93; G.D.R. 139, m. 7; below p. 32.
[5] Foss, *Judges, sub nomine;* Putnam, *Proceedings*, p. 61; *C.P.R.; C.C.R.; C.F.R.;* G.D.R. 139, m. 5d.; 215/2, m. 224; below p. 32; index, *sub nomine.*
[6] Putnam, *Proceedings*, p. 61; *C.P.R.; C.C.R.; C.F.R.; Members of Parliament; List of Sheriffs;* below p. 32.
[7] Put nam, *Proceedings*, p. 61; Bassett, *Knights of the Shire, sub nomine; C.P.R.; C.C.R.; C.F.R.; Members of Parliament; Lists of Sheriffs;* List of Escheators; below p. 32; McKisack, M., *The Fourteenth Century, 1307–1399* (Oxford, 1959), index.

Thomas de Eston was appointed justice of the peace in Bedfordshire in the commission of 21 March 1361 and also named a member of the three-man commission of 20 November 1362. According to the session headings he sat at all the sessions under the latter commission for which the names of the justices present were listed. Also it was to him that the writ of *cerciorari* of 7 June 1364 was directed. His name is a sufficiently common one so that it is uncertain whether he was the Thomas de Eston of Holme in Bedfordshire who was named tax assessor in the county in 1379. He or another of the same name was appointed justice of the peace in Hertfordshire and on various other commissions in Bedfordshire and neighbouring counties. A Thomas de Eston served as pledge for offenders indicted on Roll A.[8]

Geoffrey de Lucy (d. 1361) who had lands in Bedfordshire, Buckinghamshire, Kent, and Northamptonshire was appointed justice of the peace in Bedfordshire in 1354 and again on the 20 January 1355 commission. He was also named justice of the peace for Buckinghamshire and to the separate commissions of labourers in the two counties during these same years. He served as knight of the shire for Buckinghamshire and was named on various other commissions in both counties.[9]

John Marshall of Wootton (d. 1361), Hardwick, and Milton Ernest was first appointed justice of the peace in Bedfordshire in 1347. He was a member of the commissions of 20 January 1355 and 20 May 1356, during which time he was also named on separate commissions for labourers in both Bedfordshire and Buckinghamshire. He served Bedfordshire as knight of the shire in 1350–1351 and was on various other commissions. The mention that an offender tried by the justices of gaol delivery had been indicted before Marshall as justice of the peace indicates that he sat under one of the above commissions; he also sat as justice of gaol delivery.[10]

Sir Thomas de Reynes (d. after 1389) had land in Turvey and Thurleigh in Bedfordshire and in Buckinghamshire and Leicestershire. He was active in public affairs for many years although he does not seem to have served in one capacity for any length of time. He was justice of the peace and justice of labourers in Buckinghamshire in 1350 and knight of the shire for Buckinghamshire in 1369 and 1376–1377 and for Bedfordshire in 1370–1371. Although in 1360 he had been excused from further service against his will because of his part in the French war, he was in 1373 appointed lieutenant to the Constable of Dover Castle and Warden

[8] *C.P.R.; C.C.R.; C.F.R.;* Chancery Miscellany 47/5/125; below p. 99, nos. 21, 23, 28.
[9] Putnam, *Proceedings*, p. 61; *C.P.R.; C.C.R.; C.F.R.; Members of Parliament;* below p. 32.
[10] Putnam, *Proceedings*, p. 61; Bassett, *Knights of the Shire, sub nomine; Victoria County History, Bedfordshire,* iii, ed. by W. Page (London, 1912), pp. 147, 329; *C.P.R.; C.C.R.; C.F.R.; Members of Parliament;* G.D.R. 139, m. 5d.; 215/2,m, 71; below p. 32.

of the Cinque Ports. His name is listed first on the three-man Bedford-shire peace commission of 20 November 1362 but it is uncertain how often he sat, if at all. He was named but once in the sessions headings and the use of his name in the accounting for the fines at the exchequer may have been due to the fact that he was listed first on the peace commission.[11]

William de Riceby (d. *c.* 1388) held land at Brogborough in Bedford-shire. A man of this name was a member of the king's household, keeper of various royal properties, and a frequent recipient of grants of wine from the king. There appear in the records both William de Riceby the elder and William de Riceby the younger. It is uncertain which was justice of the peace in Bedfordshire or which held which of the offices mentioned above. Probably the one appointed justice of the peace in Bedfordshire in 1362 was also named justice of the peace in Huntingdon-shire in 1364 and was knight of the shire for Bedfordshire in 1362-1365 and for Huntingdonshire in 1366-1380. The mention of Riceby's name in the session headings on the 1363-1364 peace roll with that of Thomas de Eston may or may not indicate that he sat.[12]

John de Rokesdon who had land in Wyboston in Eaton Socon, was a member of the Bedfordshire peace commissions of 1354, 1355, and 1356 and also justice of labourers during the same period. It is probable that he sat as justice of the peace for he is mentioned with Marshall in the record of an indictment made before the justices of the peace which was before the justices of gaol delivery. Also in an entry on the pipe roll he is named with Lord Grey as having accounted for fines and amercements from the Bedfordshire sessions of the peace. Apart from the fact that he was named justice of the peace and justice of labourers in Bedfordshire nothing is known of him.[13]

Sir Peter de Salford who had land in Salford was active in Bedfordshire affairs from 1353 to 1365. In the latter year he was replaced as sheriff because in 1360 he had allowed the undersheriff to return a false jury panel. This was not his only offence, for he made a fine of 100*s.* in the King's Bench in 1357 for allowing a prisoner to escape and another of an unknown amount before the Bedfordshire justices of the peace in 1364 for a similar offence. He was appointed sheriff of Bedfordshire and Buckinghamshire in 1354-1356, 1359, and 1361-1365, escheator in 1354, justice of the peace for Bedfordshire from 1354 to 1361, justice of labourers in 1355, and he was chosen knight of the shire for Bedfordshire

---

[11] Bassett, *Knights of the Shire, sub nomine; C.P.R.; C.C.R.; C.F.R.; Members of Parliament;* Pipe Roll 210, Beds, Noua Oblata; below p. 99.

[12] Bassett, *Knights of the Shire, sub nomine; C.P.R.; C.C.R.; C.F.R.; Members of Parliament;* below p. 99.

[13] Putnam, *Proceedings,* p. 61; *Victoria County History, Bedfordshire,* iii, 192, n. 57; *C.P.R.; C.C.R.; C.F.R.;* Pipe Roll 203, Beds, Noua Oblata; G.D.R. 215/2, m. 71; below p. 32.

in 1353, 1355, 1357, 1360–1361. Perhaps the number of his offices accounted for the lapses noted above. Salford was also a victim of the assault made on Lord Grey in 1355. He appears as a witness as late as 1369; the date of his death is not known.[14]

Sir Thomas de Swyneford (d. 1361), named to the Bedfordshire peace commissions of 8 October 1355 and 20 May 1356, was a Lincolnshire man who also had lands in Bedfordshire and Buckinghamshire. He served all three counties as knight of the shire and was named to joint commissions of the peace and labourers in Bedfordshire and in the Holland division of Lincolnshire in 1350. He was escheator and sheriff of Bedfordshire and Buckinghamshire in 1344–1346 and sheriff of Rutland in the latter year.[15]

The men appointed as justices of the peace in Bedfordshire in the mid-fourteenth century were in general local men. Some of them served the county in many capacities; of others little is known. Since there is no record of the justices who actually served under the earlier commissions, it is impossible to know which justices did the work in the years covered by Roll A.

The Clerk of the Peace: As has been mentioned, the endorsement " Derby" at the end of Roll A may be the name of the man who made up the roll and who was probably clerk of the peace. No one of this name appears in any other contemporary record. Who the clerk was under the commission of 1362 is not known. As has been suggested, the differences in the two rolls would indicate that they were not the work of one man.[16]

THE SESSIONS OF THE PEACE

DATE, PLACE, AND JUSTICES PRESENT

Because there are no session headings on Roll A it provides little information about when, where, and before whom Bedfordshire sessions of the peace were held in the 1350's. References to sessions are occasionally found in cases and in the records of the King's Bench and the justices of gaol delivery. The following table summarizes what is known concerning the Bedfordshire peace sessions in the latter half of the decade.

[14] Putnam, *Proceedings*, p. 61; Bassett, *Knights of the Shire, sub nomine; C.P.R.; C.C.R.; C.F.R.; Members of Parliament; List of Sheriffs;* List of Escheators; K.B. 389, Fines, m. 2: below p. 32; p. 67, no. 93n.

[15] Putnam, *Proceedings*, p. 61; Bassett, *Knights of the Shire, sub nomine; C.P.R.; C.C.R.; C.F.R.; Members of Parliament; List of Sheriffs;* List of Escheators.

[6] Above p. 5.

	DATE	PLACE	JUSTICES NAMED AS SITTING
1356	23/30 April[1]	Bedford	
	27 July[2]	Bedford	
	26 September[3]	Bedford	
1358	8 February–12 September[4]		Lord Grey
	23 April[5]	Bedford	
	23 April–12 September[6]		John Marshall
			John de Rokesdon
	29 October[7]	Bedford	

Whether the justices sat as required by the Statute of Labourers of 1351 on Lady Day (25 March), St Margaret's Day (20 July), Michelmas (29 September), and St Nicholas Day (6 December), it is impossible to tell; they did hold sessions in the spring, the summer, and the early autumn.[8] Whether they sat in Bedford in the ' halle ' as the justices did in the fifteenth century is not known.[9] Whether Lord Grey was actually present at the sessions in connexion with which he is named, or whether he sat at all, has been considered.[10] As was suggested Marshall and Rokesdon probably sat.[11]

In 1362, before the first of the sessions recorded on Roll B, the statutory dates when sessions of the peace were to be held were made more flexible.[12] From the following table it appears that in 1363–1364, the Bedfordshire justices sat with some regularity and frequently within the statutory dates.

	DATES: Statutory	Actual	PLACE	JUSTICES NAMED AS SITTING
1363	26 February–4 March	14 March[13]	Bedford	Sir Thomas de Reynes
				William de Riceby
				Thomas de Eston
		16 March[14]	Bedford	William de Riceby
				Thomas de Eston
		13 April[15]	Biggleswade	
	21 May–24 June	25 May[16]	Bedford	William de Riceby
				Thomas de Eston
		6 June[17]	Biggleswade	
		15 July[18]	Shefford	
	29 September–6 October	2 October[19]	Bedford	William de Riceby
				Thomas de Eston
1364	6–13 January	8 January[20]	Bedford	William de Riceby
				Thomas de Eston

Again it is uncertain whether the justices named really sat. Sir Thomas de Reynes who was listed first in the commission, perhaps because he was more important than the other two members, is recorded as sitting but once, so it may be that Riceby and Eston did the bulk of the work. That justices were named only for sessions held at Bedford is interesting but probably not significant. Different clerks may have been used, or the sittings at Bedford may have been general sessions, whereas those held elsewhere were less important.[21] Undoubtedly the sittings of 14 and 16 March were part of a single session.

THE WORK OF THE SESSIONS

As has been said the two mid-fourteenth-century Bedfordshire peace rolls differ from many extant peace rolls for the later years of the century in that they record chiefly finished rather than unfinished business. Thus they give a picture of certain aspects of the work of the justices not found in some records. Also while the two rolls cover similar activities they do so in different ways.

The form of the enrolments on Roll A is such that there is recorded in a single entry all process on the offender or offenders involved in a case from presentment to conviction and punishment or acquittal. The details of process are run together and there is no clear picture of when and often how the various stages in punishing the guilty or clearing the innocent were accomplished. The omission of session headings and of any other dates except the date of an offence further conceals the sequence of events. This much is evident. In the case of a trespasser, the jury made the presentment, giving in most instances the names of the

---

[1] G.D.R. 215/2, m. 224.
[2] K.B. 388, Rex, m. 20.
[3] Below p. 61, no. 78.
[4] G.D.R. 215/2, m. 72.
[5] K.B. 388, Rex, m. 20d.
[6] G.D.R. 215/2, m. 71.
[7] Below pp. 86–87, nos. 147, 148. The sessions of 23 July 1356, 21 July 1357, and 20 July 1358 listed in Putnam, *Proceedings*, p. 58 were gaol delivery sessions. I am indebted to Mr. C. A. F. Meekings for this information.
[8] 25 Edward III, st. 2, c. 7.
[9] Putnam, *Proceedings*, p. xcvii.
[10] Above pp. 8–9.
[11] Above pp. 11, 12.
[12] 36 Edward III, st. 1, c. 12.
[13] Below pp. 102, 104. It is possible that there was a session held between the date of the receipt of the commission and the 14 March 1363 session; below pp. 102–104, no. 2.
[14] Below p. 108.
[15] Below p. 110.
[16] Below p. 112.
[17] Below p. 115.
[18] Below p. 117.
[19] Below p. 118.
[20] Below p. 120.
[21] On general sessions see Putnam, *Proceedings*, p. xcvi.

parties involved, the place, the date, and some account of the offence. The justices accepted the indictment. Those indicted were then attached for appearance, presumably at a subsequent session. If an accused appeared and admitted his guilt he made a fine, the payment of which was vouched for by, in most cases, two pledges.[22] If a man considered himself innocent he asked for and was given a jury trial which in all such instances on Roll A resulted in his acquittal.[23] There is no indication that those who were pronounced guilty had been tried or that anyone was convicted as the result of a trial. Whether the trial, if held, took place immediately on admission of guilt or at a subsequent session is not apparent. The offenders who did not appear were outlawed in the county court, presumably after five exigends or summons, and the fact of the outlawry noted at the end of the record of the indictment.[24] Whether the outlawry was formally reported at a session of the peace or was merely noted because the clerk knew it has taken place is not stated. In all, the justices heard 158 indictments for trespass which involved 211 offenders. Except for the eight whose indictments were sent to the King's Bench on a writ of November 1357, the justices of the peace tried or attempted to try all trespassers whose indictments were enrolled on Roll A.

Although it seems probable that the justices of the peace were prepared to try eleven of the twenty-two felons indicted before them, they seem to have been unable to secure the presence of any of them in court and instead received reports of their outlawry. According to the record the eleven other felons were tried by the King's Bench or the justices of gaol delivery. Because no trials of felons were held by the justices of the peace there is no record of procedure as there is for trespassers.

Roll B, which records much the same kind of business as that on Roll A, because it does so session by session gives a more complete picture of how the justices of the peace functioned. On the other hand, as will appear, it seems questionable whether there remains a complete record of all business done by the justices during the brief period, November 1362–January 1364, which the roll covers. Because the work of the justices was recorded session by session, an analysis of its contents will illustrate how the justices worked.

The earliest entry on Roll B is the commission of 20 November 1362 addressed to Reynes, Riceby, and Eston. There follows a writ of the same date which instructed Lord Grey and his associate justices under a

---

[22] For example, below p. 34, no. 2. On procedure before the justices of the peace see Putnam, *Proceedings*, pp. ciii ff.

[23] For example, below p. 36, no. 11.

[24] For example, below p. 34, no. 2. On outlawry see Holdsworth, W. S., *A History of English Law*, iii (3rd edition, rewritten, London, 1923), 604–607: Hastings, Margaret, *The Court of Common Pleas in Fifteenth Century England* (Ithaca, 1947), pp. 176–180.

previous commission, that of 21 March 1361, to turn over all records of unfinished business to the new justices.[25] It is noted that this has been done and there follows the record of two cases which presumably comprised this business. One concerned four men who had been indicted in connexion with the death of William Child, jr. The case had been in the King's Bench on appeal by Child's widow. When she failed to prosecute the appeal, the matter again came within the jurisdiction of the Bedfordshire justices of the peace and at the first session recorded on the roll, 14 March 1363 at Bedford, the sheriff was ordered to produce the four men. Three of the four appeared and were acquitted of murder. They did, however, make fines for the assault which had preceded the killing. The fourth man was to appear at a session to be held at Biggleswade on 13 April (nos. 1, 2).[26]

After a repetition of the session heading and of the writ to Lord Grey, the record of a second homicide was enrolled. Since this killing had been done in self-defence the accused had been committed to prison to await a pardon. He appeared before the justices of the peace and on producing a royal pardon was acquitted (no. 3). The justices then turned to new business and heard four presentments (nos. 4, 5, 6, 7). Although no names of jurymen were listed, the form of the entries suggests that three different juries made these presentments. The offenders were ordered to appear at subsequent sessions, 13 April at Biggleswade, 25 May at Bedford, and 6 June at Biggleswade. At a session two days later, perhaps also at Bedford since a jury from the town as well as one from the county were present, the wife of an outlawed felon was presented as his accessory and ordered to appear on 25 May (no. 8). Three trespassers previously indicted appeared and made fines and another indicted at this session was ordered to appear on 25 May (nos. 9, 10, 11). Lastly a man was indicted for felony; the clerk noted that he was gaoled and subsequently tried before the justices of the gaol delivery (no. 12). It may be added, although it does not appear on the peace roll, that he was sentenced to be hanged.[27]

At the next session held at Biggleswade on 13 April 1363, the offender who was unpunished in connexion with the death of William Child, jr., again failed to appear and the sheriff was ordered to produce him on 2 October (no. 13). Trespassers already under indictment appeared and made fines (no. 14); others who failed to appear were given a day on 6 June (no. 18); new indictments were heard and the sheriff was ordered to produce these offenders on 25 May (nos. 15, 16, 17).

On that date at Bedford some previously indicted trespassers appeared and made fines (nos. 23, 24, 25); others, both trespassers and felons,

[25] Below p. 101.
[26] See also above p. 15, n. 13.
[27] G.D.R., 223/1, m. 110.

whom the sheriff had been unable to attach, were ordered to appear on 8 January 1364. In the meantime the sheriff was instructed to initiate in the county court exaction proceedings which would culminate in outlawry should the defendants fail to appear (nos. 19, 20, 21, 22, 26). No new indictments were recorded.

When the justices met at Biggleswade on 6 June a number of trespassers appeared and made fines (nos. 27, 28), and one indictment was heard, this offender being ordered to appear on 15 July (no. 29). Previously indicted offenders who had not come were to be produced by the sheriff on 8 January 1364 and in the meantime exaction proceedings against them were to be continued (nos. 30, 31).

At Shefford on 15 July the sheriff was again ordered to produce recalcitrant offenders or continue outlawry proceedings (no. 32). Two trespassers were acquitted by jury trial (no. 33); no indictments were recorded.

At Bedford on 2 October two men who had been apprehended and charged with felonies were tried and acquitted by a jury (nos. 37, 38) as were two accused of trespass who claimed to have already made fines before Lord Grey, presumably at a session held under an earlier commission (no. 39). One trespasser appeared and was allowed to make a fine, there apparently being no need formally to indict him because he admitted his guilt (no. 36). Since the man under indictment in connexion with the death of William Child, jr., again failed to appear and since he had been exacted five times in the county court, his outlawry was reported (no. 34), and his name apparently dropped from the record. Similarly another trespasser who had been exacted five times was reported outlawed (no. 35). In this case the justices of the peace were acting on a complaint from the injured party. No indictments were recorded.

At the last session recorded on the roll, that of 8 January 1364 at Bedford, the sheriff was fined for his failure to produce two men whom he had had in his custody (no. 40). No one previously indicted appeared to make a fine or to stand trial so the outlawry of the remaining indicted but untried offenders was reported (nos. 41, 42, 43, 44). No new indictments were recorded so that as of this date no unfinished business remained, according to the roll.

In summary, in the ten months covered by the sessions on Roll B, the Bedfordshire justices of the peace heard indictments of both felons and trespassers, tried both felons and trespassers, and, although they did not find a felon guilty, received fines from trespassers. They also endeavoured through the agency of the sheriff and the threat of outlawry in the county court, to compel the appearance of indicted individuals, in many cases unsuccessfully. Not only is the roll interesting because all business recorded on it was terminated by acquittal, by fine, or by outlawry, but because many of the steps by which these ends were accomplished are carefully set out. What unfinished business, and surely the justices must have heard indictments at the later 1363 sessions which were not brought to an end either by trial or by outlawry before or at the January 1364 session, the justices passed on to their successors cannot be known.[28]

Thus, from the information on Roll B it is possible to see in some detail the operation of the process the results of which were reported on Roll A. An indicted trespasser did not commonly appear to plead innocent or make a fine at the same session at which he was indicted but at a subsequent one, and then usually on summons by the sheriff. Outlawry proceedings in the county court were initiated by the sheriff on instruction from the justices of the peace and the outlawry was reported to the justices, apparently after the outlawry had become effective. Whether or not an offender who pled guilty of trespass received a jury trial remains unanswered. Felons who pled not guilty, like trespassers, were tried by a jury.

JURIES AND PLEDGES

The clerk who made up Roll A included the jury lists and also the names of the men who served as pledges for trespassers making fines. A study of the jury lists and of the pledges yields some information about these two groups of participants in the judicial procedure. Also the roll supplies the names of a considerable number of inhabitants of Bedfordshire in the mid-fourteenth century who were neither offenders nor victims of offences. Roll B has no jury lists and no names of pledges.[29]

There are on Roll A sixty-two jury lists. Most of these contain twelve names, five thirteen, and one fourteen. Of these lists, eight are duplicates. In two instances, the names were repeated because the record of what appears to have been the same session was continued on to a new membrane. Because the enrolments were not made under session headings, there is no indication of the number of juries which presented at a given session and whether the repetition of a jury list, except in the cases mentioned, indicates a different session or a system of enrolment involving the repetition of jury lists the reason for which is not apparent. Presumably a jury composed of the same men could have presented at more than one session.

Although there is on the roll no indication of what unit within the county a given jury represented, a study of the places where offences were committed suggests that the juries can be identified with the

[28] See above p. 3.
[29] There is one jury list copied from the record of the indictment in the death of William Child, jr. (no. 1), and the names of four mainpernors appear in connexion with the imprisonment and pardon in the second homicide case (no. 3). As these men did not appear at the sessions recorded on the peace roll they are not included in the discussion which follows.

hundreds. These identifications are strengthened by the fact that jurors who served more than once seem to have represented the same hundred. For what it is worth, the following list has been compiled. Although it may not be completely accurate, it probably does indicate the general distribution of the juries among the nine Bedfordshire hundreds and the town of Bedford. For ease of identification juries have been numbered in footnotes to the text of the roll. Parentheses indicate a jury list repeated on a new membrane. Identical juries are starred. One uncertain identification is queried.

HUNDRED		
Barford	7, 30*, 44, 48*, 51 ?, 55	6
Biggleswade	4 (5), 10* (11), 18*, 25, 34, 41, 45, 53, 61	9 (11)
Clifton	19*, 24*, 31, 58	4
Flitt	2, 13, 20, 28	4
Manshead	1, 12, 16, 23, 62	5
Redbornstoke	21*, 38, 60*	3
Stodden	6, 14, 22, 27, 33, 39, 40, 49, 54, 57	10
Willey	29, 42, 50	3
Wixamtree	3, 9, 15, 26, 35*, 37*, 43, 46, 52*, 56*	10
Bedford, town	8, 17, 32, 36, 47, 59	6
		60 (62)

In addition to the 314 men on these juries, there were approximately two hundred who served as pledges for offenders making fines before the justices of the peace. Inasmuch as several men served in both capacities, jurors and pledges may be considered together. The following figures are not exact, as few men are identified on the roll by their place of residence or by their occupation, so that what appears to have been the same man serving twice or in two capacities may have been two men of the same name each serving once. Of the approximately 450 men, the majority, 250, served but once, 153 as jurors, 97 as pledges. Approximately forty jurors served twice as did about the same number of pledges. Only a few served frequently.[30] A man might serve as a pledge for his servant (nos. 9, 30), for a co-offender (no. 88), for another offender apparently making a fine at the same session (no. 89), or for the man who had injured him (no. 16). A man not infrequently served as pledge for someone presented by the jury on which the pledge was serving (nos. 129, 136), and the same man or men might serve for several offenders who may have appeared at the same session (nos. 91, 92; 106, 107, 108).[31] Chaplains and other religious occasionally served as pledges (nos. 65, 77, 85).

[30] For example, John Freynshe, Richard Ledere, index, *sub nomine*.
[31] It is uncertain whether indictment and fine took place at the same session; above p. 16.

Although for most jurors and pledges nothing beyond a name is known, for a few more information is available. Of the 450, about thirty held one or more positions of some importance. Eight were knights of the shire for Bedfordshire or sat in parliament for the town;[32] eleven or twelve were coroners;[33] eleven, tax collectors;[34] seven, justices of the peace;[35] and two, royal bailiffs.[36] The appearance of coroners as jurors and pledges was not unusual, for coroners were required to attend the sessions of the peace and while there might well have acted in a second capacity.[37] Benedict Blundel, coroner for Bedfordshire from June 1350 to July 1359, served five times as juryman and four times as pledge, probably while he was coroner.[38] Whether the tax collectors or the royal bailiffs were in court on business is not known. The justices of the peace were not under appointment to the office during the period when they served as jurors.

THE OFFENCES ON THE PEACE ROLLS

The indictments before the justices of the peace in mid-fourteenth-century Bedfordshire afford some information concerning the type of offences being committed and so provide some slight picture of conditions in the county during the period. This picture is very incomplete because the periods covered by the two rolls are brief and because, without doubt, the crimes recorded on the rolls were but a fraction of those committed

---

[32] Bedfordshire: Sir John Bekeryng; Bassett, *Knights of the Shire, sub nomine; Members of Parliament.* Bedford: John Boryate, Robert Carbommel, Richard Frereman, William de Kempston, John Knottyng, Thomas Peyntour, John Salford; *Members of Parliament.*

[33] Dunstable: John Aungevyn, Thomas Nicol. Bedford: Robert Carbommel, Richard Frereman. Bedfordshire, northern district: Henry de Bereford, John Hervy, William Mordant. (There were two William Mordants, junior and senior, who served on juries. Whether one of them served twice as coroner, or each of them once is uncertain.) Bedfordshire, southern district: Benedict Blundel, John Child. Bedfordshire, district unknown: John Pertesoil, John Sporoun; *Bedfordshire Coroners' Rolls*, ed. R. F. Hunnisett (Bedfordshire Historical Record Society, Publications, xli, Streatley, 1961), pp. xxxviii–xlv; below pp. 118–119, 121–123, nos. 34, 35, 41, 42, 43, 44.

[34] John Blundel, Alexander Boyoun, Robert de Ipre, William Laurence, Simon Loryng, John Malyng, William Mordant, jr., William Mordant, sr., John atte Park, Thomas Stepynglee, Sir Alexander Stopesleye; *C.F.R., sub nomine;* below p. 83, no. 138.

[35] Alexander Boyoun (1364), Richard Crannfeld (1368), Thomas de Eston (1361, 1362), John FitzJohn (1361), John Malyng (1368), John de Middilton (1368), William de Otford (1361), *C.P.R., sub nomine;* above pp. 7–11.

[36] Roger Garkyn, Thomas le Sock: below p. 78, no. 125; p. 84, no. 140.

[37] Hunnisett, R. F., *The Medieval Coroner (Cambridge Studies in English Legal History,* Cambridge, 1961), pp. 97, 188, n. 5.

[38] Hunnisett, *Bedfordshire Coroners' Rolls*, p. xi; below, index, *sub nomine.*

in the years covered. The offences for which indictments were brought fall into the two general categories known to criminal law as felonies and trespasses. Because of the nature of the material on the peace rolls an exact classification or numerical count of offences or offenders is not possible. Often several persons were accused of the same offence, some of them not being named. A single indictment might involve more than one offence. Also offences were not always described in terms which are meaningful today. In assigning categories to offences and in compiling figures for each type, the following practices have been followed.

Offences, not offenders or cases, have been counted. In determining whether an individual had committed more than one offence the criterion of separate presentment has been used. The figures therefore refer neither to individuals, because a man might be accused of more than one offence or more than one man be involved in a single offence, nor to entries because often offences committed on different dates were handled together, perhaps because the offender answered for them all at the same session.

Duplicate entries of the same indictment have been counted but once.

A breach of the peace involving more than one offence has been catalogued under what seems to have been considered, according to the wording of the indictment, the principal or more serious offence.

An indictment for general lawlessness which follows an indictment for a specific offence has not been counted.

A further caveat must be added. For some offenders who appear on Roll B no specific offence is named because they had been indicted at a previous peace session and the entry on the roll refers only to a summons or an appearance in court. These offences, since they cannot be catalogued, have not been counted. They are too few in number to have added materially to the totals for the types of offences.

Even with these qualifications the classification and counting of offences is uncertain, partly because the juries or the clerks were not always consistent or detailed in their descriptions of what happened, and partly because it is difficult to decide on the most suitable classification for some offences.

FELONIES

Petty treason: A, 1 instance. Petty treason as defined by the statute of 1352 comprised the slaying of a master by his servant, a husband by his wife, or a prelate by his subject.[1] A man and a woman were indicted for killing the woman's husband (A, no. 152). No mention of the special nature of the crime was made in the indictment. The offenders did not appear for trial and were outlawed.

---

[1] 25 Edward III, st. 5, c. 2; see also Blackstone, W., *Commentaries on the Laws of England* (12th edition, 1795), iv, 202–204.

Homicide: A, 5 instances; B, 3 instances. In one case homicide was preceded by robbery (A, no. 100); in another robbery followed the killing (A, no. 95). Homicide sometimes resulted from an assault and might, therefore, not have been intentional. In one case two officials attempted to make an attachment on an offender. After the latter had refused to discuss the matter and his servants had come to his support, one of the officials was killed (A, no. 75). It is not clear from the wording of the indictment whether the servants were indicted as accessories. In another case one of two men assaulted was killed (B, nos. 1, 2). In both instances the widows initiated appeals but failed to follow through on them. Both indictments were summoned to chancery. Nothing is recorded of the outcome of the first case; in the second, because the appeal was dropped, the indictment was returned to the justices of the peace for action. Three of the accused who appeared for trial were cleared of the homicide charge but made fines for the assault.[2] Two killings were said to have been done in self-defence; one offender produced a pardon and was acquitted (B, no. 3); the other did not appear for trial and was outlawed (B, no. 29). Since pardons were not difficult to obtain if one had the wherewithal, the accused may have thought that a plea of self-defence would not stand up in court or he may have lacked the money or influence to secure the necessary document.[3]

Larceny: A, 11 instances; B, 5 instances. In only one of these cases (B, no. 37) was the larceny petty larceny as the value of the stolen goods was less than 12*d.* Whether some of these cases should be classified as burglary is unclear. Although the verb, *burgare,* was not used and only once was the offence committed at night, an offender might break in before stealing (A, no. 128). The verb, *fregere,* was perhaps used to indicate that the theft was committed indoors. Articles stolen included horses, a saddle, sheep, cloth, and money. Once a pix valued at 100*s.* was taken from a church (A, no. 134).

Robbery: A, 4 instances; B, 1 instance. This offence was designated by the verb, *depredare.* Twice, as has been noted, homicide was involved; horses were the goods most commonly taken.

Accessories: A, 3 instances; B, 2 instances. Accessories had aided men guilty of homicide or had received stolen goods which were, in one instance, sold (A, no. 137). If a principal was outlawed and the accessory pled not guilty he was acquitted (A, nos. 137, 177). If an accessory, like the principal, failed to appear for trial he too was outlawed (A, no. 100; B, no. 16).

[2] Above p. 17.
[3] On pardons see *The Shropshire Peace Roll, 1400–1414,* ed. by E. G. Kimball (The Shropshire County Council, Shrewsbury, 1959), pp. 43–45.

TRESPASSES

Trespasses fall into two categories: common-law trespasses and those committed in violation of the economic regulations including the labour laws. Common-law trespasses which were usually described as committed *contra pacem* or *vi et armis* may be further divided into those which, because violence was involved, were semi-criminal in nature, miscellaneous trespasses, and trespasses against officials and the government. The period covered by Roll A is the period during which the government was experimenting with separate justices of labourers to enforce the labour legislation.[4] Consequently the few economic offences, with one exception, are found on Roll B. The great majority of trespasses on both rolls were common-law trespasses against individuals or officials.

Assault: A, 99 instances; B, 10 instances. By far the larger number of trespasses on both rolls fall into this category. Assaults usually involved beating and wounding. Sometimes the assault took place at night and frequently the offender was described as a common disturber of the peace. Assault was accompanied by the taking of goods in Biggleswade market (A, no. 22), abduction, imprisonment of the victim, and extortion (A, nos. 51, 102), threats and extortion (A, no. 69), threats which made a man afraid to leave his house (A, no. 119), and pursuit with a drawn knife (A, no. 122), once to a church (B, no. 25). An assault was sometimes premeditated (B, no. 27) and, as has been noted, it might lead to homicide. Accessories to assaults were treated as principals as were all accessories to trespasses (A, nos. 123, 135, 142).

Battery and fighting: A, 23 instances; B, 1 instance. Offences of this type seem to have been distinguished from assaults chiefly in the wording of the indictments which do not contain the phrase *insultum fecit*, but specify only wounding or beating or both. Often the victim was in danger of death. Two men involved in a fight were both indicted (B, no. 10). In one instance, a man and his wife beat and wounded another man and his wife (A, no. 23).

Taking goods: A, 7 instances. This offence resembled larceny and how a jury distinguished between the two is not made clear. In one instance, twenty sheep were taken (A, no. 43). In another one hundred newly branded oxen and sheep were taken from the servants of the prior of Dunstable; both cattle and servants were injured (A, no. 92). One offender broke up and carried away hedges from a close (A, no. 157).

Abduction: A, 3 instances. A wife was abducted (A, no. 13) as was a servant (A, no. 32). The case of a maidservant dragged from her master's

---

[4] Putnam, B. H., *Enforcement of the Statute of Labourers* (Columbia University, Studies in History, Economics and Public Law, xxxii, New York, 1908), pp. 7 ff.

house and rescued by a chaplain who made a fine for her release may be an example of intended abduction or intended rape (A, no. 29).

Threatened rape: A, 1 instance.

Waylaying and threatening: A, 7 instances; B, 1 instance. The nature of the threats was frequently not specified. Sometimes men lay in wait with intent to kill and persisted in doing so over a considerable period of time (A, no. 132).

Vagrancy and disturbing the peace: A, 12 instances. Whether or not these offences involved violence is uncertain for juries did not always describe what nightwanderers were doing (A, no. 45), nor are victims mentioned. Frequenters of taverns sometimes became riotous (A, no. 44).

Offences against officials: A, 20 instances; B, 1 instance. These offences which run the gamut of common-law trespasses include assaults, threats, resistance to arrest, escaping the custody of a constable, and releasing men in custody. If attachment was resisted, the indictment for so doing might be recorded as part of the indictment for the offence for which the attachment was being made (A, no. 25). One man who had been ordered into service by the justices of labourers broke attachment (A, no. 35). Three men attached by order of the justices of the peace broke arrest but were subsequently rearrested and appeared to make fines for so doing (A, nos. 37, 56, 76). The case of the official killed while attempting to make an arrest has been mentioned. Constables were the most frequent victims of these offences but bailiffs, royal and manorial, had their difficulties as did bailiffs of tax collectors (A, nos. 138, 139) and jurors, two of whom were assaulted because they had served in this capacity (A, nos. 40, 113).

Offences in court: A, 3 instances. These offences consisted of attacking another with a weapon in the presence of the justices of the peace; one man drew blood (A, nos. 78, 147, 148). That such episodes became more frequent is suggested by the serious riot which took place before the Bedfordshire justices of the peace in the fifteenth century.[5] The assault on Lord Grey, although it did not take place in court, shows similar disrespect for the king's justices.[6]

The few miscellaneous trespasses provide interesting indictments. For some of them the lack of detailed information, particularly about motive, is tantalizing.

[5] Putnam, *Proceedings*, p. cxi; see also above p. 9.
[6] Above p. 9.

3

Ejecting a lessee: A, 1 instance. The prior of Chicksands was indicted for ejecting two tenants. He was acquitted on showing that he had acted within the terms of the lease since their rent was in arrears (A, nos, 12, 18).

Cutting down trees: A, 1 instance. This offender had three times entered a wood, cut down and carried away eighty oak and ash trees, and broken hedges in order to make a way. He appeared in court, admitted his guilt, and made his fine (A, no. 20). One wonders how he expected to succeed in such a project unless the road was so badly needed that he expected his neighbours to approve. Since the amount of the fine was 5*s.*, perhaps he made enough to pay it by selling the wood he had cut.

Rescuing cattle: A, 1 instance. The reason why the cattle had been taken is not given (A, no. 64).

Revealing counsel: A, 2 instances. These indictments involved jurymen who were accused of revealing the counsel of the king and of their fellow jurors in violation of their juryman's oath.[7] One was acquitted and served again at what may have been a later date (A, no. 90); the other made a fine (A, no. 130).

False purveyance: A, 2 instances. These offenders falsely posed as royal purveyors; in one case geese, capons, and cocks were taken from various people under false pretences (A, no. 173); in the other, three men, one of whom was a stranger, took sheep, or money in lieu of sheep, from a number of victims (A, no. 175).

As has been said the few indictments for offences against the labour laws appear chiefly on Roll B because separate justices of labourers were functioning during the years covered by the earlier roll.

Abduction of servants: A, 1 instance. This case which is on Roll A would properly seem to have been within the competence of the justices of labourers because the man was abducted from service he had sworn to do (A, no. 57). As some of the same men were appointed as both justices of labourers and justices of the peace in Bedfordshire, perhaps they used the same clerk who made a mistake in making the enrolment.[8]

Leaving employment: B, 1 instance. A shepherd became a roofer, whether because the pay was higher is not stated (B, no. 5).

---

[7] *Some Sessions of the Peace in Lincolnshire, 1360–1375*, ed. by R. Sillem (Lincoln Record Society, *Publications*, 30, Hereford, 1937), pp. xxxvii–xxxviii.
[8] Above pp. 10, 11, 12, 13.

Charging excess prices: B, 2 instances. Tanners sold tanned hides for 4*d.* in the shilling in excess of the legal price (B, nos. 33, 39).

Taking excess wages: B, 2 instances. Excess wages were taken for sowing grain and in an unspecified occupation (B, nos. 6, 7).

The figures above may be summarized as follows:

Felonies	35
Common-law trespasses	195
Economic trespasses	6
	236

As has been pointed out these offences were mostly crimes of violence, all the felonies and practically all the common-law trespasses answering to this description. It is probable that this picture of crime in mid-fourteenth-century Bedfordshire is incomplete. No doubt many economic offences were brought before the justices of labourers for whom no records exist. Similarly if the extant records of the justices of the peace covered a longer period, miscellaneous trespasses which were not always violent in nature might have been more numerous so that the percentage of assaults would not have been so large. Among those indicted there seems to have been only an occasional hardened offender. One such was Edmund Pulter of Caddington who was indicted for various assaults, for threatening, and for taking goods (A, no. 62). There were some ' common malefactors ' but in the main there was comparatively little repetition of offences by the same person within the admittedly short period covered by the rolls. That there was lawlessness in Bedfordshire in the middle years of the fourteenth century is evident; that the situation differed from that in other parts of the country is not apparent.

THE PUNISHMENT OF OFFENDERS

As has been pointed out, the records of the mid-fourteenth-century Bedfordshire justices of the peace are concerned chiefly with completed business. It may therefore be pertinent to see what was the outcome of the indictments which the justices heard. Of the twenty-four felons whose indictments appear on Roll A, eleven were outlawed for failure to appear for trial, presumably before the justices of the peace since no mention is made of any other jurisdiction and the outlawry in the county court was recorded on the peace roll. Eight felons having been imprisoned came before the justices of gaol delivery; of these, five were acquitted, a sixth was acquitted but imprisoned again for another offence, a seventh was convicted and having pled clergy was released to the ordinary, and the eighth acquitted by the justices of gaol delivery was subsequently judged guilty in the King's Bench. He pled clergy and was released to the ordinary. Five, in addition to the one already mentioned, were brought before the King's Bench. Of these one was judged guilty and sentenced to be hanged (no. 95), another against whom an appeal was lodged but not prosecuted, was exacted and presumably outlawed for failure to appear (no. 75). The other three were acquitted, one of these being an accessory whose principal had been outlawed.

Of the fourteen felons whose records appear on Roll B, six were acquitted by the justices of the peace, one being released on a pardon; a seventh was sentenced to be hanged by the justices of gaol delivery and six were outlawed in the county court for failure to appear before the justices of the peace. The fourteenth, a woman, was reported too ill to appear in court.

Thus of a total of thirty-eight felons, two were sentenced to be hanged, two were judged guilty but pled clergy, fifteen were acquitted although one of these was remitted to prison for another offence, and nineteen did not appear for trial. Unless many of these indictments did not represent actual offences, serious offenders seem to have gone unpunished. Certainly the Bedfordshire justices of the peace tried few and of those they did try they sentenced no one.

Their record in the punishment of trespassers appears better in that they were able to secure the appearance of the great majority of the trespassers for whom indictments are recorded on the two peace rolls. Of the 211 offenders whose indictments are found on Roll A, 178 appeared. Of these 170 apparently pled guilty for they made fines; the other eight were acquitted. Twenty-six failed to appear and their outlawry in the county court was reported on the peace roll. One of these subsequently appeared before the King's Bench and made a fine, his outlawry having been judged insufficient. Of seven others whose indictments went before the King's Bench, two made fines and the rest were presumably outlawed since they were in exigend for failure to appear. That the fines were paid is attested by records on the pipe rolls. For the years 30–32 Edward III, Michelmas 1356–Michelmas 1358, and again in 34 Edward III, Michelmas 1359–Michelmas 1360, Lord Grey and his associates accounted at the exchequer for £57–0–2.[1] The fines noted on the peace roll tally to £60–10–4. It is not to be expected that the sums would agree inasmuch as the years covered by the records on the peace roll are not known exactly. Also the justices may have deducted expenses, if not wages, before turning in their fines.[2]

---

[1] Pipe Roll 203, 205, Beds, Noua Oblata.
[2] Putnam, *Proceedings*, pp. lxxxix ff.

Of the forty-two trespassers for whom indictments are recorded on Roll B, thirty-one appeared before the justices, twenty-six to admit guilt and make fines, five to plead innocent and be acquitted. Two were reported as having been outlawed for failure to appear, and one who had been in the custody of the sheriff escaped. As the amounts of the fines were not recorded on the peace roll, no total of the fines is known. Reynes and his associate justices accounted at the exchequer for 37 Edward III, Michelmas 1362–Michelmas 1363, for £69–17–6.[3] This sum, exceedingly large as compared with the fines for the earlier years, suggests that the justices did business not recorded on the peace roll. The fines do not include money received in the years between 1359 and 1362 because Lord Grey had accounted for £92–14–9 for 35–36 Edward III, Michelmas 1360–Michelmas 1362.[4] There is no question but that justice was a profitable business in Bedfordshire in the middle of the fourteenth century.[5]

This picture of the punishment of offenders is much the same as that for other counties in the fourteenth century.[6] Trespassers appeared and if guilty made fines which, in general, they seem to have paid. Felons, on the other hand, did not appear in any large numbers. In view of the small percentage of convictions among those who did appear, it would seem the felon had little reason to fear punishment. The alternative to appearance, outlawry, was not effective as a means of enforcing appearance. At the most it occasioned some inconvenience unless mobility was so great that a man did not mind leaving his own neighbourhood to settle in one where hopefully his past would not catch up with him.

SUMMARY

Because of the brief period covered by the two Bedfordshire peace rolls printed in this volume and the rather limited character of the offences, the peace rolls do not provide an extensive picture of conditions in the county in the middle of the fourteenth century. That there was much

[3] Pipe Roll 210, Beds, Noua Oblata.

[4] Ibid., 208, Beds, Noua Oblata.

[5] Putnam, *Proceedings*, pp. lxxxix ff.; *The Place in Legal History of Sir William Shareshull*, pp. 72 ff.

[6] Putnam, *Proceedings*, pp. cxxvii–cxxviii; Sillem, *Some Sessions of the Peace in Lincolnshire, 1360–1375*, pp. xlvii–1; Kimball, *Rolls of the Gloucestershire Sessions of the Peace, 1361–1398*, p. 49; *The Shropshire Peace Roll*, pp. 41–45; *Some Sessions of the Peace in Lincolnshire, 1381–1396*, I, li–lviii; *Essex Sessions of the Peace, 1351, 1377–1379*, ed. by E. C. Furber (Essex Archaeological Society, *Occasional Publications*, 3, Colchester, 1953), pp. 55–60; *Rolls of the Warwickshire and Coventry Sessions of the Peace, 1377–1397*, ed. by E. G. Kimball (Dugdale Society, *Publications*, XVI, London, 1939), pp. lxix–lxxiii.

lawlessness is evident from the large number of assaults for which indictments were made. But there is no reason to think that the situation was worse in Bedfordshire than elsewhere in England. Nor is there any reason to conclude that crime in Bedfordshire consisted largely of crimes of violence. As has been pointed out separate justices of labourers were functioning during much of the period covered by the peace rolls, so that indictments for labour offences which often provide information about employment, wages, prices, and other economic matters are scarce. The lack of indictments for thefts, which cannot be taken as evidence that few were committed, means there is little information about the type of goods stolen and so about the values of goods.

The financial information which does appear is found in the fines which were assessed and, on the evidence of returns to the exchequer, paid. Fines ranging from 6*d.* to 40*s.* were made and nearly two hundred and twenty pounds were paid into the exchequer in eight years. It is difficult to determine what this tells of economic conditions in fourteenth-century Bedfordshire because there is little information about fines beyond their amounts. Rather there are several unanswerable questions. Were fines made in accordance with the seriousness of an offence and if so why did not everyone involved in a single offence or in offences which appear to have been comparable, fine for the same amount? Did the amount of a fine depend upon previous conviction, reputation, ability to pay? The Bedfordshire peace rolls do not provide answers for these questions. Whether they can be answered from a comparative study of similar records for other counties or from other records for Bedfordshire is a question outside the scope of this study. In any case, the amounts paid coupled with the apparent willingness to pay do not indicate financial stringency.

As has been pointed out, there are on these rolls a large number of names of inhabitants of Bedfordshire in the middle of the fourteenth century. Because the indictments on Roll A, in addition to the offender or offenders and the victim or victims, contain the names of pledges and because some sixty odd juries, usually of twelve men, were listed, the genealogist should find here valuable information. Unfortunately most men were not identified by their places of residence and for few were there occupational designations. The latter circumstance coupled with the paucity of economic offences leaves one with no sense of what most of the people named on the rolls did for a living. That they were men attached to the land rather than transients cannot be argued solely from lack of evidence to the contrary.

Whether the place-name specialist will find anything unusual or interesting in the names on the rolls is doubtful.

Thus, in conclusion, it may be said that these rolls, interesting as they are for the light they throw on judicial procedure before the justices of the peace in the mid-fourteenth century, do not in themselves throw much light on conditions in Bedfordshire. Perhaps the local historian will find in them material to use in conjunction with other material to add to his knowledge of fourteenth-century Bedfordshire.

SESSIONS OF THE PEACE,

1355-1359

ROLL A

ASSIZE ROLL 32

[m.1]

Placita coram Reginaldo de Grey de Ruthyn et socijs suis iusticiarijs domini regis ad audiendum et terminandum assignatis virtute commissionis eisdem directe in hec verba.

Edwardus dei gracia rex Anglie et Francie et dominus Hibernie dilectis et fidelibus suis Reginaldo de Grey de Ruthyn Gerardo de Braybrok' Roberto de Thorp' Hugoni de Sadelyngstanes Galfrido de Lucy Iohanni Mareschal de Wotton' Petro de Salford' Iohanni de Rokesdon' et Iohanni Dardern' salutem. Sciatis quod assignauimus vos coniunctim et diuisim ad pacem nostram necnon ad statuta apud Wynton' et Norhampton' pro conseruacione pacis eiusdem edita in omnibus et singulis suis articulis in comitatu Bed' tam infra libertates quam extra custodienda et custodiri facienda; et ad omnes illos quos contra formam statutorum predictorum delinquentes inueneritis castigandos et puniendos prout secundum formam statutorum eorundem fuerit faciendum; et ad ordinandum superuidendum et faciendum quod omnes et singuli homines in comitatu predicto infra libertates(et[1]) extra iuxta eorum status et facultates armis competentibus muniantur arraientur et parentur et de incedendo et auxiliando vobis et cuilibet vestrum in hijs que pacis et statutorum predictorum conseruacionem concernunt ipsos compellendos prout melius fore videbitur expedire. Assignauimus eciam vos octo septem sex quinque quatuor tres et duos vestrum iusticiarios nostros ad inquirendum per sacramentum proborum et legalium hominum de comitatu predicto tam infra libertates quam extra per quos rei veritas melius sciri poterit de quibuscumque felonijs et transgressionibus in eodem comitatu infra libertates vel extra per quoscumque et qualitercumque factis; et ad omnes huiusmodi transgressiones ad sectam nostram tantum audiendas et terminandas secundum legem et consuetudinem regni nostri Anglie; et ad processus versus omnes quos de felonijs huiusmodi contigerit indictari quousque capiantur reddantur vel vtlagentur faciendos. Assignauimus eciam vos octo septem sex quinque quatuor tres et duos vestrum quorum alterum vestrum vos prefati Roberte et Hugo vnum esse volumus iusticiarios nostros ad felonias predictas audiendas et terminandas et ad omnia indictamenta feloniam tangencia coram vobis iam vltimo assignatis facta ac processus de huiusmodi felonijs coram vobis nondum terminata; ac eciam vos octo septem sex quinque quatuor tres et duos vestrum iusticiarios nostros ad omnia alia indictamenta feloniam non tangencia coram vobis facta ac processus de eisdem nondum terminata debito fine terminanda secundum legem et consuetudinem supradictas. Et ideo vobis mandamus quod ad certos dies et loca quos vos octo septem sex quinque quatuor tres vel duo vestrum ad hoc prouideritis inquisiciones super premissis ac processus huiusmodi faciatis et premissa omnia et singula audiatis et terminetis in forma predicta facturi inde quod ad iusticiam pertinet secundum legem et consuetudinem regni nostri Anglie saluis nobis amerciamentis et alijs ad nos inde spectantibus. Mandauimus enim vicecomiti nostro comitatus predicti quod ad certos dies et loca quos vos octo septem sex quinque quatuor tres vel duo vestrum ei scire faciatis venire faciat coram vobis octo septem sex quinque quatuor tribus vel duobus vestrum tot et tales probos et legales homines de balliua sua tam infra libertates quam extra per quos rei veritas in premissis melius sciri poterit et inquiri. In cuius rei testimonium has litteras nostras fieri fecimus patentes. Teste me ipso apud Westm' xx die Ianuarij anno regni nostri Anglie vicesimo octauo regni vero nostri Francie quintodecimo [1355]. (*Marg.* Bed')

1. Walterus Picot[1] Willelmus Burcestre Alexander Appelee Iohannes Salford' Iohannes Porter Henricus Hussebourne Willelmus Conquest Iohannes Morton' Henricus Skapelory Willelmus Offencote Radulfus Staleworth' et Thomas Wrast' dicunt per sacramentum suum quod Reginaldus filius Iohannis de Merston' die annunciacionis beate Marie anno regni regis nunc tricesimo apud Euersholt vi et armis insultum fecit Iohanni Iordan de Rugemond et ipsum verberauit et vulnerauit contra pacem. Qui quidem Iohannes attachiatus fuit ad respondendum domino regi et fecit finem et dat domino regi x s. per plegium Iohannis Salford Thome Wrast et Willelmi Fencote. (*Marg.* finem x s.)

Reginald son of John de Merston, at Eversholt, assaulted John Jordan of Ridgmont, beating and wounding him; being attached, he made a fine for 10s.; pledges, John Salford, Thomas Wrast, William Fencote.

2. Dicunt eciam quod Robertus Dawe Robertus Clerk' et Garinus filius Gilberti Muleward de Appelegise die Lune proxima ante festum sancti Georgij anno regni regis nunc tricesimo apud Appelegise insultum fecerunt noctanter Michelo Scot' de Woubourne et ipsum verberauerunt et vulnerauerunt contra pacem. Item dicunt quod dictus Robertus Clerk' est communis perturbator pacis. Qui quidem Robertus Dawe et Garinus

[1]Jury 1.

attachiati fuerunt ad respondendum domino regi et dictus Robertus Dawe fecit finem et dat domino regi xxx s. per plegium Thome Dawes et Radulfi Crannfeld et dictus Garinus fecit finem et dat domino regi xiij s. iiij d. per plegium Thome Wrast et Willelmi Fencote. Et dictus Robertus Clerk positus fuit in exigendis et per processum exactus de comitatu in comitatum quousque vtlagatus fuit. (*Marg.* finem xxx s. finem xiij s. iiij d. vtlagatus)

Robert Dawe, Robert Clerk, and Garinus son of Gilbert Muleward of Aspley Guise, at Aspley Guise, at night assaulted Michel Scot of Woburn, beating and wounding him. Robert Clerk is a disturber of the peace. Being attached, Robert Dawe made a fine for 30s.; pledges, Thomas Dawes, Ralph Crannfeld; Garinus, a fine for 13s. 4d.; pledges, Thomas Wrast, William Fencote. Robert Clerk was exacted and outlawed.

3. Dicunt eciam quod Ricardus Fille de Appelee die Sabati proxima ante festum annunciacionis beate Marie anno regni regis nunc tricesimo insultum fecit Thome atte Welle de Appelee constabulario domini regis et Agneti vxori sue et ipsos verberauit et vulnerauit contra pacem. Qui quidem Ricardus attachiatus fuit ad respondendum domino regi et fecit finem et dat domino regi ijs. per plegium Ricardi Wrighte et Iohannis Staleworth'. (*Marg.* finem ij s.)

Richard Fille of Aspley assaulted Thomas atte Welle of Aspley, king's constable, and Agnes his wife, beating and wounding them; being attached, he made a fine for 2s.; pledges, Richard Wrighte, John Staleworth.

4. Dicunt eciam quod Iohannes Peyntour de Eueresholt die Veneris proxima ante festum sancti Petri aduincula anno regni regis nunc vicesimo nono apud Woubournechapel insultum fecit Thome Fauconner de Appelegise et ipsum verberauit et vulnerauit contra pacem. Dicunt eciam quod idem Iohannes Peyntour de Eueresholt circa festum natiuitatis sancti Iohannis Baptiste anno regni nunc vicesimo nono apud Eueresholt insultum fecit Radulfo Clerk in domo sua et ipsum verberauit et vulnerauit contra pacem. Qui quidem Iohannes attachiatus fuit ad respondendum domino regi et fecit finem et dat domino regi xx s. per plegium Iohannis Bekeryng chiualer et Walteri de Mershston'. (*Marg.* finem xx s.)

John Peyntour of Eversholt, at Woburn Chapel, assaulted Thomas Fauconner of Aspley Guise, beating and wounding him; he also assaulted Ralph Clerk in his house at Eversholt, beating and wounding him; being attached, he made a fine for 20s.; pledges, John Bekeryng, Kt., Walter de Mershton.

5. Dicunt eciam quod Thomas Holenden de Leighton' circa festum sancti Petri aduincula anno regni nunc vicesimo nono apud Woubourne-chapel insultum fecit Thome Yoman de Dunstapel et ipsum verberauit et vulnerauit contra pacem. Qui quidem Thomas Holenden attachiatus fuit ad respondendum domino regi et fecit finem et dat domino regi xxvj s. viij d. per plegium Iohannis Child et Iohannis Longcroft. (*Marg.* xxvj s. viij d.)

Thomas Holenden of Leighton, at Woburn Chapel, assaulted Thomas Yoman of Dunstable, beating him and wounding him; being attached, he made a fine for 26s. 8d.; pledges, John Child, John Longcroft.

6. Dicunt eciam quod Petrus Olyue de Rugemond circa festum sancti Petri aduincula anno regni regis nunc vicesimo nono apud Rugemond insultum fecit Thome Beuyn? de eadem et ipsum verberauit et vulnerauit contra pacem et est communis perturbator pacis. Qui quidem Petrus attachiatus fuit ad respondendum domino regi et fecit finem et dat domino regi vj s. viij d. per plegium Ricardi de Nortwode et Iohannis Lecke. (*Marg.* finem vj s. viij d.)

Peter Olyve of Ridgmont, at Ridgmont, assaulted Thomas Bevyn? of Ridgmont, beating and wounding him; he is a common disturber of the peace; being attached, he made a fine for 6s. 8d.; pledges, Richard de Nortwode, John Lecke.

7. Dicunt eciam quod Iohannes Donnyng de Weston circa festum annunciacionis beate Marie anno regni regis nunc tricesimo apud Weston' insultum fecit Henrico Skapelori de eadem et ipsum verberauit et vulnerauit contra pacem. Qui quidem Iohannes attachiatus fuit ad respondendum domino regi et fecit finem et dat domino regi xl d. per plegium Petri Smyth' et Willelmi Smyth'. (*Marg.* finem xl d.)

John Donnyng of Westoning, at Westoning, assaulted Henry Skapelori of Westoning, beating and wounding him; being attached, he made a fine for 40d.; pledges, Peter Smyth, William Smyth.

8. Ricardus de Faldho[1] Willelmus Abbot Hugo atte Spytel Willelmus Fullere Iohannes La Wele iunior Iohannes Aungewyn Adam Messager Hugo atte Welle Willelmus Belleuerge Ricardus Mile Iohannes Cranewelle et Iohannes Sharphenho dicunt per sacramentum suum quod Alexander de Bray de Luton die Dominica proxima post festum annunciacionis beate Marie anno regni regis nunc tricesimo apud Luton' venit vi et armis et ibidem obuiam Willelmo Wyot et Henrico Wyot insultum fecit et ipsos

[1] Jury 2.

verberauit et male tractauit contra pacem et est communis malefactor. Qui quidem Alexander attachiatus fuit ad respondendum domino regi et fecit finem et dat domino regi vj s. viij d. per plegium Alexandri de Stopesleye chiualer et Willelmi Canuylle. (*Marg.* finem vj s. viij d.)

Alexander de Bray of Luton, at Luton, waylaid and assaulted William Wyot and Henry Wyot, beating and maltreating them; he is a common malefactor; being attached, he made a fine for 6s. 8d.; pledges, Alexander de Stopesleye, Kt., William Canvylle.

9. Dicunt eciam quod Galfridus Aylmar seruiens Thome Ikebid de Luton et Iohannes Muleward de Luton smyth' pugnauerunt vagantes et discurrunt contra pacem. Qui quidem Galfridus attachiatus fuit ad respondendum domino regi et fecit finem et dat domino regi xl d. per plegium Hamonis le Clerk et Thome Ikebid. Et dictus Iohannes Muleward positus fuit in exigendis et per processum exactus de comitatu in comitatum quousque vtlagatus fuit. (*Marg.* finem xl d. vtlagatus)

Geoffrey Aylmar servant of Thomas Ikebid and John Muleward of Luton smith are vagrants and fighters; being attached, Geoffrey made a fine for 40d.; pledges, Hamo le Clerk, Thomas Ikebid. John Muleward was exacted and outlawed.

10. Dicunt eciam quod Ricardus Gayteys et Willelmus Taillour vagantes et discurrunt contra pacem. Qui quidem Willelmus attachiatus fuit ad respondendum domino regi et fecit finem et dat domino regi ij s. per plegium Roberti de Ipre et Iohannis Oliueyre. Et dictus Ricardus positus fuit in exigendis et per processum exactus de comitatu in comitatum quousque vtlagatus fuit. (*Marg.* finem ij s. vtlagatus)

Richard Gayteys and William Taillour are vagrants: being attached, William made a fine for 2s.; pledges, Robert de Ipre, John Oliveyre. Richard was exacted and outlawed.

[*m. 1d.*]
11. Dicunt eciam quod Bartholomeus capellanus Alexandri de Stoppeslee militis die Iouis proxima post festum inuencionis sancte crucis anno regni regis nunc tricesimo insultum fecit Thome de Wendulborgh' et eum verberauit contra pacem. (Qui quidem Bartholomeus[i]) attachiatus fuit ad respondendum domino regi de transgressione predicta qui dicit quod in nullo est culpabilis et de hoc ponit se super patriam. Ideo capiatur inde iurata que dicit quod in nullo est culpabilis. Ideo eat inde quietus. (*Marg.* quietus)

Bartholomew chaplain of Alexander de Stoppeslee, Kt., assaulted Thomas de Wendulborgh and beat him; being attached, he pled not guilty; the jury acquitted him.

12. Dicunt eciam quod Iohannes Lechworth' prior de Chekesonde cum alijs ignotis die Lune proxima post festum sancti Thome apostoli anno regni regis nunc vicesimo nono venit vi et armis apud Meperteshale ad manerium vocatum Seint Thomas chapel et ibidem inuenerunt bona et catalla ad valenciam lx li. Willelmi Prat et Nicholai atte Halle qui habuerunt dictum manerium ad firmam de dicto priore et conuentu et eos eiecerunt et catalla detinuerunt contra pacem. Qui quidem Iohannes attachiatus fuit ad respondendum domino regi de transgressione predicta qui dicit quod Rogerus predecessor suus manerium predictum dimisit predictis Nicholao et Willelmo ad certum terminum reddendo sibi et successoribus suis annuatim xxx quarteria bladorum ad festum omnium sanctorum sub tali condicione quod quandocumque bladum predictum ad terminum predictum in parte vel in toto aretro fuerit quod bene liceret sibi et successoribus suis manerium predictum cum omnibus bonis et catallis in eodem inuentis ingredi seysire et retinere imperpetuum. Et quia x quarteria bladorum predictorum ad terminum predictum aretro fuerunt intrauit ipse manerium predictum et seisiuit cum pace et non contra pacem vt ei bene licuit. Et hoc paratus est verificare prout curia considerauerit in hac parte. Ideo capiatur inde iurata que dicit quod Rogerus predecessor prioris nunc manerium predictum dimisit eisdem Nicholao et Willelmo sub condicione et forma quibus prior nunc per placitum allegauit et quod predictus prior quia x quarteria redditus predicti ad terminum predictum aretro fuerunt intrauit ipse et seisiuit manerium predictum et catalla predicta cum pace et non contra pacem et absque iniuria alicui facienda. Ideo dictus prior eat inde quietus. (*Marg.* quietus)

John Lechworth, prior of Chicksands, with others unknown, at Meppershall, entered the manor called St Thomas Chapel, took goods valued at £60, and ejected William Prat and Nicholas atte Halle who held the manor at farm from the said prior and convent. Being attached, John said that Roger, his predecessor, had let the manor to the said Nicholas and William for a certain term for 30 quarters of grain to be paid on All Saints' Day with the right to repossess the manor should the rent in whole or part be in arrears. Because the rent was in arrears 10 quarters, he had taken possession of the manor. The jury confirmed the prior's statement and acquitted him. See below no. 18.

13. Dicunt eciam quod Iohannes Tokebury die Iouis proxima post festum annunciacionis beate Marie anno regni regis nunc tricesimo venit apud Luton' ad domum Rogeri Grenewey et abduxit vxorem dicti Rogeri

contra pacem. Qui quidem Iohannes attachiatus fuit ad respondendum domino regi de transgressio predicta qui dicit quod in nullo est culpabilis et de hoc ponit se super patriam. Ideo capiatur inde iurata que dicit quod in nullo est culpabilis. Ideo eat inde quietus. (*Marg.* quietus)

John Tokebury coming to the house of Roger Grenewey at Luton abducted Roger's wife; being attached, he pled not guilty; the jury acquitted him.

14. Benedictus Blundel[1] Willelmus Burcestre Iohannes Buddenho Walterus Picot Willelmus Freynshe Robertus Holewelle Robertus Tymcok' Iohannes atte March' Iohannes Ordwy Iohannes Bateman Nicholaus Taillour et Iohannes Passewater dicunt per sacramentum suum quod Iohannes Cartere taillour de Caldecote est perturbator pacis de eo quod fecit rescussum domine Matilli de Trumpeton' et balliuis suis multociens per tres annos elapsos et bis fregit parcum domini regis et ter fregit parcum dicte Matillis super attachiamentum factum pro seruicio domini regis et pro redditu dicte Matillis et insultum fecit balliuis dicte Matillis et manus in eos posuit ad verberandum et postea congregauit socios suos vi et armis ad incidiandum balliuum dicte Matillis contra pacem. Qui quidem Iohannes attachiatus fuit ad respondendum domino regi de transgressione predicta qui dicit quod in nullo est culpabilis et de hoc ponit se super patriam. Ideo capiatur inde iurata que dicit quod in nullo est culpabilis. Ideo eat inde quietus. (*Marg.* quietus)

John Cartere tailor of Caldecote is a disturber of the peace who resisted Lady Matilda de Trumpeton and her bailiffs many times in the last three years, twice broke into the king's park, and three times into that of Lady Matilda; he resisted attachment for services due the king and rent due Lady Matilda; he assaulted her bailiffs and with his friends threatened one of them; being attached, he pled not guilty; the jury acquitted him.

15. Dicunt eciam quod Robertus Heryng de Fenlake apud Fenlake verberauit et male tractauit Iohannem de Bramhton' de Bikeleswade contra pacem. Item dicunt quod idem Robertus insultum fecit Iohanni Laictropage messori abbatisse de Elnestowe et eum verberauit contra pacem. Item dicunt quod idem Robertus insultum fecit Willelmo Gurnard et sagittauit eidem contra pacem. Qui quidem Robertus attachiatus fuit ad respondendum domino regi et fecit finem et dat domino regi xiij s. iiij d. per plegium Roberti Boynoun et Rogeri Ril. (*Marg.* finem xiij s. iiij d.)

Robert Heryng of Fenlake, at Fenlake, beat and maltreated John de Bramhton of Biggleswade; he assaulted and beat John Laictropage, hayward of the abbess of Elstow; he assaulted William Gurnard and shot at him; being attached, he made a fine for 13s. 4d.; pledges, Robert Boynoun, Roger Ril.

[1]Jury 3.

16. Dicunt eciam quod Robertus Ologon de Mogerhanger insultum fecit Roberto Tymcok' balliuo ducis Lancastre et optulit se pugnare cum dicto Roberto Tymcok' contra pacem. Qui quidem Robertus Ologon attachiatus fuit ad respondendum domino regi et fecit finem et dat domino regi xl d. per plegium Roberti Tymcok' et Walteri atte Brigge. (*Marg.* finem xl d.)

Robert Ologon of Mogerhanger assaulted Robert Tymcok bailiff of the duke of Lancaster and fought with him; being attached, he made a fine for 40d.; pledges, Robert Tymcok, Walter atte Brigge.

17. Item dicunt quod idem Robertus minabatur constabularijs villate de Mogerhanger quod non (sunt¹) ausi facere officium suum. Qui quidem Robertus attachiatus fuit ad respondendum domino regi et fecit finem vt supra.

The same Robert threatened the constables of Mogerhanger so that they did not dare to perform their office; being attached, he made a fine as above.
See above no. 16.

18. Dicunt eciam quod Iohannes de Lectheworth' prior de Chekesonde cum alijs ignotis in manerium vocatum Seint Thomas chapel intrauit et bona et catalla Willelmi Prat de Bed' et Nicholai atte Halle de Stotfolde ibidem inuenta ad valenciam centum solidorum ceperunt et asportauerunt contra pacem. Qui quidem Iohannes attachiatus fuit ad respondendum domino regi de transgressione predicta qui dicit quod Rogerus predecessor suus manerium predictum dimisit predictis Nicholao et Willelmo ad certum terminum reddendo sibi et successoribus suis annuatim xxx quarteria bladorum ad festum omnium sanctorum sub tali condicione quod quandocumque bladum predictum ad terminum predictum in parte vel in toto aretro fuerit quod bene liceret sibi et successoribus suis manerium predictum cum omnibus bonis et catallis in eodem inuentis ingredi seysire et retinere imperpetuum. Et quia x quarteria bladorum predictorum ad terminum predictum aretro fuerunt intrauit ipse manerium predictum et seisiuit cum pace et non contra pacem vt ei bene licuit et hoc paratus est verificare prout curia considerauerit in hac parte. Ideo capiatur inde iurata que dicit quod Rogerus predecessor prioris nunc manerium predictum dimisit eisdem Nicholao et Willelmo sub condicione et forma quibus prior nunc per placitum allegauit et quod predictus prior quia x quarteria redditus predicti ad terminum predictum aretro fuerunt intrauit ipse et seisiuit manerium predictum et catalla predicta cum pace cepit et asportauit et non contra pacem et absque iniuria alicui facienda. Ideo predictus prior eat inde quietus. (*Marg.* quietus)

See above no. 12.

19. Dicunt eciam quod Thomas Bicok' tannator prioris de Chekesonde die Lune in festo sancti Edmundi archiepiscopi anno regni regis Edwardi nunc vicesimo nono in campis del Brom in hundredo de Wixt' felonice interfecit Willelmum Louelay de le Brom. Et dictus Thomas positus fuit in exigendis et per processum exactus de comitatu in comitatum quousque vtlagatus fuit. (*Marg.* vtlagatus)

Thomas Bicok tanner of the prior of Chicksands, in Broom meadow in Wixamtree hundred, feloniously killed William Lovelay of Broom; he was exacted and outlawed.

20. Dicunt eciam quod Willelmus Gurnay de Harwedon' intrauit boscum Willelmi de Pateshull' apud Kerdyngton' per tres vices et iiij^{xx} quercos et fraxinos succidit et cum carecta sua asportauit et fregit sepes dicti bosci ad faciendum viam vbi via prius non erat contra pacem domini regis et voluntatem dicti Willelmi de Pateshull'. Qui quidem Willelmus Gurnay attachiatus fuit ad respondendum domino regi et fecit finem et dat domino regi v s. per plegium Walteri Picot et Willelmi Clerk'. (*Marg.* finem v s.)

William Gurnay of Harrowden entered the wood of William de Pateshull at Cardington three times and cut down and carried away in his cart 80 oak and ash trees; he broke the hedges of the wood to make a road where previously there had been none; being attached, he made a fine for 5s.; pledges, Walter Picot, William Clerk.

21. Radulfus Beuchamp[1] Willelmus Laurence Iohannes Wodhull' Thomas Nicohol Adam de Kent' Iohannes Letice Robertus Pustel Iohannes Freynshe Iohannes Sneterle Iohannes Whyte Willelmus Richema' (et[1]) Iohannes Bramhton' dicunt per sacramentum suum quod Willelmus de Rothewelle de Cetteworthe die Lune proxima post festum inuencionis sancte crucis anno regni regis Edwardi nunc tricesimo apud Dunton' insultum fecit Iohanni le Iay de Dunton' et ipsum verberauit vulnerauit et male tractauit contra pacem. Qui quidem Willelmus attachiatus fuit ad respondendum domino regi et fecit finem et dat domino regi xl d. per plegium Thome de Eston' et Iohannis Norice. (*Marg.* finem xl d.)

William de Rothewelle of Edworth, at Dunton, assaulted John le Jay of Dunton, beating, wounding, and maltreating him; being attached, he made a fine for 40d.; pledges, Thomas de Eston, John Norice.

22. Dicunt eciam quod Iohannes Albon de Stanford die Lune proxima post festum sancti Ambrosij anno regni regis Edwardi tercij tricesimo in mercato de Bikeleswade insultum fecit Andree seruienti Willelmi le Smyth' de Tadelowe et quamdam mantellam precij vj s. viij d. de eo vi et

---

[1]Jury 4.

armis eripuit et asportauit iniuste et contra pacem domini regis et ad dampnum ipsius Andree xx s. et alia enormia ei intulit videlicet mappas eius disrupit et vlteria prefato Andree maximas minas coniecit de vita et membris eius. Qui quidem Iohannes attachiatus fuit ad respondendum domino regi et fecit finem et dat domino regi xiij s. iiij d. per plegium Iohannis Oliuer' et Rogeri Garkyn. (*Marg.* finem xiij s. iiij d.)

John Albon of Stanford in the market of Biggleswade assaulted Andrew servant of William le Smyth of Tadlowe [Cambs] and snatched from him a mantle, price 6s. 8d.; he inflicted damage to the amount of 20s. and threatened Andrew's life; being attached, he made a fine for 13s. 4d.; pledges, John Oliver, Roger Garkyn.

[*m.2*]
23. Radulfus Beuchamp[1] Willelmus Laurence Iohannes Wodhull' Thomas Nicohol Adam de Kent Iohannes Letice Robertus Pustel Iohannes Freynshe Iohannes Sneterle Iohannes Whyte Willelmus Richeman et Iohannes Bramhton' dicunt per sacramentum suum quod Willelmus Maggesson' de Dunton' et Custancia vxor Willelmi de Rothewelle die Lune proxima post festum inuencionis sancte crucis anno regni regis Edwardi nunc tricesimo venerunt ad domum Iohannis Iay de Dunton' et ibidem Agatham vxorem dicti Iohannis Iay predicti Willelmus et Custancia verberauerunt vulnerauerunt et male tractauerunt contra pacem. Qui quidem Willelmus et Custancia attachiati fuerunt ad respondendum domino regi et dictus Willelmus fecit finem et dat domino regi xl d. per plegium Ricardi Maggesson et Willelmi Laurence et dicta Custancia fecit finem et dat domino regi xl s. [*sic*] per plegium Thome de Eston' et Iohannis Norice. (*Marg.* finem xl d. finem xl d.)

William Maggesson of Dunton and Custancia wife of William de Rothewelle came to the house of John Jay of Dunton and beat, wounded, and maltreated Agatha, his wife; being attached, each made a fine for 40d.; pledges for William, Richard Maggesson, William Laurence; for Custancia, Thomas de Eston, John Norice.

24. Dicunt eciam quod Iohannes Bethewater de Sandeye die Sabati proxima post festum sancti Dionisij anno regni regis nunc vicesimo nono apud Sandeye noctanter insultum fecit Emme Reignold et eam verberauit vulnerauit et male tractauit contra pacem. Qui quidem Iohannes attachiatus fuit ad respondendum domino regi et fecit finem et dat domino regi xiij s. iiij d. per plegium Willelmi Colleuylle et Iohannis Malynz. (*Marg.* finem xiij s. iiij d.)

John Bethewater of Sandy, at Sandy, at night assaulted Emma Reignold, beating, wounding, and maltreating her; being attached, he made a fine for 13s. 4d.; pledges, William Collevylle, John Malynz.

[1]Jury 5.

4

25. Dicunt eciam quod die Dominica proxima post festum sancti Laurencij anno regni regis nunc vicesimo nono apud Bikeleswade quidam extraneus insultum fecit Roberto Waryn et idem percussit preteria constabularij venerunt ad attachiandum predictum extraneum et predictus extraneus fugebat ad domum Thome le Sock' et dictus Thomas noluit pati ipsum attachiari set rescussum fecit constabularijs dicte ville contra pacem. Qui quidem Thomas attachiatus fuit ad respondendum domino regi et fecit finem et dat domino regi xl d. per plegium Thome Child et Iohannis Golde. (*Marg.* finem xl d.)

At Biggleswade an unknown man assaulted Robert Waryn; when the constables came to arrest him, the man took refuge with Thomas le Sock who refused to give him up and resisted the constables; Thomas, being attached, made a fine for 40d.; pledges, Thomas Child, John Golde.

26. Dicunt eciam quod Willelmus Richardyn de Bikeleswade die Dominica proxima post festum conuersionis sancti Pauli anno regni regis nunc vicesimo nono vulnerauit Walterum Drawe et Walterum Shepherde contra pacem. Qui quidem Willelmus attachiatus fuit ad respondendum domino regi et fecit finem et dat domino regi xl d. per plegium Willelmi Child et Roberti Warde. (*Marg.* finem xl d.)

William Richardyn of Biggleswade wounded Walter Drawe and Walter Shepherde; being attached, he made a fine for 40d.; pledges, William Child, Robert Warde.

27. Dicunt eciam quod Ricardus Hurton' die Lune proxima post festum sancti Nicholai anno regni regis nunc vicesimo octauo apud Bikeleswade vulnerauit Adam atte Grene de le Brom. Et Ricardus Steuenes de Holme fuit abettor ad hoc contra pacem. Qui quidem Ricardus et Ricardus attachiati fuerunt ad respondendum domino regi et dictus Ricardus Hurton' fecit finem et dat domino regi x s. per plegium Willelmi Freynshe et Rogeri Garkyn et dictus Ricardus Steuenes fecit finem et dat domino regi xl d. per plegium predictorum Willelmi et Rogeri. (*Marg.* finem x s. finem xl d.)

At Biggleswade Richard Hurton abetted by Richard Stevenes of Holme wounded Adam atte Grene of Broom; being attached, Richard Hurton made a fine for 10s., Richard Stevenes for 40d.; pledges, William Freynshe, Roger Garkin.

28. Dicunt eciam quod Iohannes Estwyk' in vigilia pasche anno regni regis nunc tricesimo verberauit Agnetem Freisel contra pacem. Qui quidem Iohannes attachiatus fuit ad respondendum domino regi et fecit finem et dat domino regi xl d. per plegium Willelmi Otford et Thome Eston'. (*Marg.* finem xl d.)

John Estwyk beat Agnes Freisel; being attached, he made a fine for 40d.;
pledges, William Otford, Thomas Eston.

29. Dicunt eciam quod Robertus Basset est communis perturbator pacis
et quod dictus Robertus et Rogerus Corbat die Lune proxima post
festum sancti Luce anno regni regis nunc vicesimo octauo intrauerunt
clausum Alani Muleward contra voluntatem suam et ancillam suam
tractauerunt extra clausum contra pacem. Et dominus Henricus Muleward capellanus venit ad adiuuandum dictam ancillam et dicti Robertus
et Rogerus verberasse voluerunt dictum Henricum nisi fecisset finem
videlicet vj s. viij d. et finem soluit predictis Roberto et Rogero. Qui
quidem Robertus attachiatus fuit ad respondendum domino regi et fecit
finem et dat domino regi xxvj s. viij d. per plegium Iohannis Estwik' et
Willelmi Mustel. Et dictus Rogerus positus fuit in exigendis et per
processum exactus de comitatu in comitatum quousque vtlagatus fuit.
(*Marg.* xxvj s. viij d. vtlagatus)

Robert Basset is a common disturber of the peace; he and Roger Corbat
entered the close of Alan Muleward and dragged out his maidservant;
when Henry Muleward chaplain came to her aid they threatened to beat
him unless he made a fine with them for 6s. 8d., which he did; being
attached, Robert made a fine for 26s. 8d.; pledges, John Estwik, William
Mustel; Roger was exacted and outlawed.

30. Dicunt eciam quod Iohannes seruiens Roberti Warde de Bikeleswade
die Mercurij proxima post festum purificacionis beate Marie virginis
anno regni regis nunc vicesimo septimo verberauit dominum Willelmum
capellanum contra pacem et eodem (die[i]) et anno supradictis dictus
Iohannes minas fecit constabularijs dicte ville. Qui quidem Iohannes
attachiatus fuit ad respondendum domino regi et fecit finem et dat
domino regi ij s. per plegium Willelmi Child et Roberti Warde. (*Marg.*
finem ij s.)

John servant of Robert Warde of Biggleswade beat William, the chaplain;
he also threatened the constables of Biggleswade; being attached, he made
a fine for 2s.; pledges, William Child, Robert Warde.

31. Dicunt eciam quod Rogerus le Smyth' de Potton' die Martis
proxima post festum purificacionis beate Marie virginis anno regni regis
Edwardi tricesimo apud Potton' vulnerauit Iohannem Letice contra
pacem. Qui quidem Rogerus attachiatus fuit ad respondendum domino
regi et fecit finem et dat domino regi xiij s. iiij d. per plegium Roberti
Pustel et Iohannis Sneterlee. (*Marg.* finem xiij s. iiij d.)

Roger le Smyth of Potton, at Potton, wounded John Letice; being attached,
he made a fine for 13s. 4d.; pledges, Robert Pustel, John Sneterlee.

32. Dicunt eciam quod Robertus Horlee de Potton' die Lune proxima post festum sancti Iohannis ante portam latinam anno regni regis Edwardi tercij vicesimo octauo verberauit Galfridum Laxton' contra pacem. Item quod idem Robertus die Martis proxima post Dominicam in ramis palmarum anno regni regis Edwardi tercij tricesimo [sic] nono verberauit Iohannem Gery. Item quod idem Robertus die Veneris in vigilia assumpcionis beate Marie anno regni regis Edwardi tercij vicesimo nono verberauit Walterum Clement contra pacem. Qui quidem Robertus attachiatus fuit ad respondendum domino regi et fecit finem et dat domino regi xx s. per plegium Iohannis Letice et Iohannis Sneterlee. (*Marg.* finem xx s.)

Robert Horlee of Potton beat Geoffrey Laxton, John Gery, and Walter Clement; being attached, he made a fine for 20s.; pledges, John Letice, John Sneterlee.

33. Dicunt eciam quod Henricus Babyngton' de Temesford' die Mercurij proxima post festum sancti Barnabe apostoli anno regni regis Edwardi tercij vicesimo nono verberauit Iohannem Louel et vulnerauit vxorem suam contra pacem. Qui quidem Henricus attachiatus fuit ad respondendum domino regi et fecit finem et dat domino regi v s. per plegium Hugonis Bray et Iuonis Reignold. (*Marg.* finem v s.)

Henry Babyngton of Tempsford beat John Lovel and wounded his wife; being attached, he made a fine for 5s.; pledges, Hugh Bray, Ivo Reingold.

34. Dicunt eciam quod Willelmus Gernoun iunior et Willelmus Robyn de Eddeworthe sunt communes perturbatores pacis. Qui quidem Willelmus et Willelmus attachiati fuerunt ad respondendum domino regi et dictus Willelmus Gernoun fecit finem et dat domino regi xl d. per plegium Willelmi Mustel et Iohannis de Kent. Et dictus Willelmus Robyn fecit finem et dat domino regi xl d. per plegium predictum. (*Marg.* finem xl d. finum xl d.)

William Gernoun, jr., and William Robyn of Edworth are common disturbers of the peace; being attached, they each made a fine for 40d.; pledges, William Mustel, John de Kent.

35. Iohannes Pertesoil[1] Ricardus Ledere Willelmus Iurdan Thomas Mause Rogerus le Deen Iohannes Ichyngton' Willelmus Waukeleyn Iohannes Reigner Robertus Gardiner Robertus Trate Iohannes Bolle et Iohannes Cole turnour dicunt per sacramentum suum quod Willelmus Bongent de Suldrop die Sabati proxima post festum sancti Dunstani anno regni regis Edwardi tercij tricesimo apud Suldrop attachiatus fuit per Iohannem Muryman balliuum domini regis per preceptum iusticiariorum

[1]Jury 6.

domini regis de operatoribus ad seruiendum Willelmo Betheree de Suldrop sicut iuratus fuit coram dictis iusticiarijs de statuto predicto apud Rislee et dictus Willelmus Bongent eodem die fregit attachiamentum predictum contra pacem. Qui quidem Willelmus positus fuit in exigendis et per processum exactus de comitatu in comitatum quousque vtlagatus fuit. (*Marg.* vtlagatus)

William Bongent of Souldrop, at Souldrop, was attached by John Muryman, king's bailiff, on order of the justices of labourers to serve William Betheree of Souldrop as he had sworn to do before the justices at Riseley; he broke the attachment and was exacted and outlawed.

36. Dicunt eciam quod Stephanus le Heir de Pertenhale capellanus et Iohannes le Heir frater dicti Stephani die Dominica proxima post festum sancti Martini anno regni regis Edwardi tercij vicesimo nono apud Pertenhale noctanter insultum fecerunt Thome de Beuerelee et ipsum verberauerunt et vulnerauerunt contra pacem. Qui quidem Stephanus et Iohannes attachiati fuerunt ad respondendum domino regi et dictus Stephanus fecit finem et dat domino regi xx s. per plegium Willelmi Oyldeboef et Stephani de Holecote. Et dictus Iohannes fecit finem et dat domino regi xx s. per plegium predictum. (*Marg.* finem xx s. finem xx s.)

Stephan le Heir of Pertenhall, chaplain, and John le Heir, his brother, at night, at Pertenhall, assaulted Thomas de Beverelee, beating and wounding him; being attached, they each made a fine for 20s.; pledges, William Oyldeboef, Stephan de Holecote.

37. Dicunt eciam quod Iohannes le Eyr de Pertenhale die Martis proxima ante festum sancti Augustini anno regni regis Edwardi tercij tricesimo apud Pertenhale attachiatus fuit per Iohannem de Ichyngton' per preceptum Reginaldi de Grey et sociorum suorum iusticiariorum domini regis de pace in comitatu Bed' ad respondendum domino regi de comtemptibus et transgressionibus diuersis et eodem die dictus Iohannes le Eyr fregit attachiamentum contra pacem et sic noluit se iustificari ad pacem. Qui quidem Iohannes attachiatus fuit ad respondendum domino regi et fecit finem et dat domino regi vj s. viij d. per plegium Willelmi Oyldeboef et Stephani le Smyth'. (*Marg.* finem vj s. viij d.)

John le Eyr of Pertenhall, at Pertenhall, was attached by John de Ichyngton on order of Reginald de Grey and his associates, justices of the peace, to answer for various trespasses; he broke the attachment and refused to swear to keep the peace; being attached, he made a fine for 6s. 8d.; pledges, William Oyldeboef, Stephan le Smyth.

38. Dicunt eciam quod Iohannes le Soutere de Rislee iunior circa festum inuencionis sancte crucis anno regni regis Edwardi tercij vicesimo nono

apud Risle insultum fecit Iohanni Barkere de eadem et ipsum verberauit et vulnerauit contra pacem et est communis perturbator pacis. Qui quidem Iohannes attachiatus fuit ad respondendum domino regi et fecit finem et dat domino regi v s. per plegium Iohannis Pertesoil et Iohannis Cole. (*Marg.* finem v s.)

John le Soutere of Riseley, jr., at Riseley, assaulted John Barkere of Riseley, beating and wounding him; he is a common disturber of the peace; being attached, he made a fine for 5s.; pledges, John Pertesoil, John Cole.

[*m. 2d.*]
39. Dicunt eciam quod Iohannes de Holecote de Pertenhale Galfridus Parkere Willelmus le Parkere de Brighthamwyk' Dauid Careles et Alanus Ionysman de Holecote die Lune in festo sancti Gutlacij anno regni regis Edwardi tercij tricesimo apud Pertenhale vi et armis intrauerunt clausum Willelmi le Eyr et ipsum Willelmum le Eyr et Galfridus le Smyth' verberauerunt et male vulnerauerunt et mahemiauerunt Willelmum le Eyr. Qui quidem Iohannes de Holecote attachiatus fuit ad respondendum domino regi et fecit finem et dat domino regi xl s. per plegium Roberti de Hammes et Iohannis Astel. Et predicti Galfridus Willelmus le Parkere Dauid et Alanus positi fuerunt in exigendis et per processum exacti de comitatu in comitatum quousque vtlagati fuerunt. (*Marg.* finem xl s. vtlagati)

John de Holecote of Pertenhall, Geoffrey Parkere, William le Parkere of Brighthamwick [Hunts], David Careles, and Alan Jonysman of Holcote, at Pertenhall, forcibly entered the close of William le Eyr, wounded him and Geoffrey le Smyth, and maltreated and maimed William le Eyr; John de Holecote, being attached, made a fine for 40s.; pledges, Robert de Hammes, John Astel; the other four were exacted and outlawed.

John de Holecote to be produced before the King's Bench, Trinity 1357 and subsequently, to answer concerning a trespass against William le Eyr, whence Holecote had been convicted in the King's Bench; K.B. 388, Rex, m. 4d.; 389, Rex, m. 7.

40. Ricardus Beuchamp[1] Willelmus Picot Henricus de Bereford' Iohannes Blundel Iohannes Pirpard Willelmus Mordant iunior Ricardus Englys Thomas Saltere Robertus le Lord Willelmus Merlyn Thomas Baa et Elias Smyth' dicunt per sacramentum suum quod Ricardus Mustard de Ronhale venit cum gladijs et fustibus et alijs armis contra pacem per noctem et diem et intrauit domum Simonis Lord contra voluntatem ipsius Simonis et insultum ei fecit et ipsum voluit occidere quia fuit in inquisicione domini regis inter Willelmum Picot et Ricardum Mustard. Qui quidem Ricardus attachiatus fuit ad respondendum domino regi et

[1]Jury 7.

fecit finem et dat domino regi v s. per plegium Walteri Picot et Simonis Maydelot. (*Marg.* finem v s.)

Richard Mustard of Renhold coming armed by night and day entered the house of Simon Lord, assaulted him, and tried to kill him because Simon was on a jury in a case between William Picot and Richard; being attached, he made a fine for 5s.; pledges, Walter Picot, Simon Maydelot.

41. Dicunt eciam quod Iohannes Neyroun de Rauenesden' venit contra pacem cum gladijs et fustibus per noctem et diem et vxorem suam habuit in await et ipsam voluit occidere et quia Ricardus Archer ipsam voluit adiuuare insultum fecit dicto Ricardo et ipsum verberauit contra pacem. Qui quidem Iohannes attachiatus fuit ad respondendum domino regi et fecit finem et dat domino regi x s. per plegium Ricardi Shepherde et Willelmi Driuere. (*Marg.* finem x s.)

John Neyroun of Ravensden armed day and night lay in wait to kill his wife and because Richard Archer came to her aid, he assaulted and beat him; being attached, he made a fine for 10s.; pledges, Richard Shepherde, William Drivere.

42. Dicunt eciam quod Iohannes Pulter die Lune proxima ante festum sancti Andree apostoli anno regni regis Edwardi tercij vicesimo nono apud Wilden' felonice furatus fuit tres oues precij iij s. de Nicholao Soor et iij oues precij iij s. (de Iohanne^c) de Iohanne Wrighte. Qui quidem Iohannes Pulter captus fuit et in prisona detentus quousque deliberatus fuit coram Roberto de Thorp'. (*Marg.* coram Roberto de Thorp')

John Pulter, at Wilden, feloniously stole 3 sheep, price 3s., from Nicholas Soor, and 3 sheep, price 3s., from John Wrighte; he was released from gaol by Robert de Thorp.
    Acquitted, delivery Bedford gaol, 23 July 1356; G.D.R. 139, m. 5d.; 215/2, m. 224.

43. Dicunt eciam quod Ricardus Chamburleyn venit vi et armis et cepit viginti oues de Willelmo Colet de Wilden' contra voluntatem suam et contra pacem. Qui quidem Ricardus attachiatus fuit ad respondendum domino regi et fecit finem et dat domino regi v s. per plegium Iacobi de Pabenham chiualer et Alexandri Boyoun. (*Marg.* finem v s.)

Richard Chamburleyn forcibly took 20 sheep from William Colet of Wilden; being attached, he made a fine for 5s.; pledges, James de Pabenham, Kt., Alexander Boyoun.

44. Dicunt eciam quod Willelmus Tolouse et Iohannes Hunte et socij sui vtuntur tabernam per noctem et diem et sunt communes perturbatores pacis et si constabularij volunt ipsos attachiare nolunt se iustificari. Qui

quidem Willelmus attachiatus fuit ad respondendum domino regi et fecit finem et dat domino regi ij s. per plegium Iohannis prioris de Bysshemade et dictus Iohannes positus fuit in exigendis et per processum exactus de comitatu in comitatum quousque vtlagatus fuit. (*Marg.* finem ij s. vtlagatus)

William Tolouse, John Hunte, and others frequent taverns by night and day and are common disturbers of the peace; they resist attachment by the constables; William, being attached, made a fine for 2s.; pledge, John prior of Bushmead; John Hunte was exacted and outlawed.

45. Dicunt eciam quod Ricardus Chommessone iuit per noctem contra pacem et est communis perturbator pacis. Qui quidem Ricardus positus fuit in exigendis et per processum exactus de comitatu in comitatum quousque vtlagatus fuit. (*Marg.* vtlagatus)

Richard Chommessone wandered at night and is a common disturber of the peace; he was exacted and outlawed.

46. Dicunt eciam quod Willelmus Coupere de Rokesdon' vi et armis intrauit in domum et in clausum Iohannis Fraunk' et contra voluntatem suam asportauit bona et catalla et contra pacem. Qui quidem Willelmus attachiatus fuit ad respondendum domino regi et fecit finem et dat domino regi xl d. per plegium Iohannis Coupere et Walteri Dekene. (*Marg.* finem xl d.)

William Coupere of Roxton forcibly entered the house and close of John Fraunk and carried away goods and chattels; being attached, he made a fine for 40d.; pledges, John Coupere, Walter Dekene.

47. Dicunt eciam quod Nicholaus Picot die Lune proxima post festum sancti Nicholai anno regni regis Edwardi tercij vicesimo nono apud Wilden' intrauit domum Ricardi Wygod et cepit unum lectum ad valenciam xl d. contra pacem. Qui quidem Nicholaus positus fuit in exigendis et per processum exactus de comitatu in comitatum quousque vtlagatus fuit. (*Marg.* vtlagatus)

Nicholas Picot, at Wilden, entered the house of Richard Wygod and took a bed valued at 40d.; he was exacted and outlawed.

48. Robertus Carbommel[1] Henricus Shareman Robertus Bele Hugo Lauche Thomas Spicer Walterus Gosefot Willelmus Crowe Iohannes Daubour Iohannes Knottyng Adam Yerdelee Willelmus Rauenesden' et Iohannes Forster dicunt per sacramentum suum quod Willelmus le Rook die Mercurij proxima ante festum Pasche anno regni regis nunc vicesimo octauo apud Bed' felonice furatus est unam scellam equitaturam precij

[1] Jury 8.

v s. de Iohanne le Wayte et est communis malefactor. Qui quidem Willelmus captus fuit et in prisona detentus quousque deliberatus fuit coram Roberto de Thorp'. (*Marg.* coram Roberto de Thorp')

William le Rook, at Bedford, feloniously stole a saddle, price 5s., from John le Wayte; he is a common malefactor; he was released from gaol by Robert de Thorp.

Acquitted, delivery Bedford gaol, 23 July 1356; G.D.R. 139, m. 5d.; 215/2, m. 224; returned to prison for another offence and released to manucaptors; ibid.*; see below no. 172.*

49. Dicunt eciam quod Iohannes Tannere de Mildulton' Erneys Iohannes filius Rogeri le Fleyshewere et Rogerus frater eius cum multis alijs ignotis die Martis in festo inuencionis sancte crucis anno regni regis nunc tricesimo venerunt apud Bed' insultum fecerunt Alicie que fuit vxor Iohannis Daberoun militis et quemdam Ricardum le Reue eodem tempore verberauerunt vulnerauerunt et male tractauerunt et eodem tempore predictus Rogerus sagittauit quemdam Iohannem Feukens garconem Willelmi Croysere contra pacem. Qui quidem Iohannes Iohannes et Rogerus attachiati fuerunt ad respondendum domino regi et dictus Iohannes Tannere fecit finem et dat domino regi xl d. per plegium Philipi Erneys et Iohannis Bettelowe et dictus Iohannes filius Rogeri fecit finem et dat domino regi xl d. per plegium predictum et dictus Rogerus frater eius fecit finem et dat domino regi xl d. per plegium predictum. (*Marg.* finem xl d. finem xl d. finem xl d.)

John Tannere of Milton Ernest, John son of Roger le Fleyshewere, and his brother Roger, with others unknown, at Bedford, assaulted Alice widow of John Daberoun, Kt., and Richard le Reve, beating, wounding, and mal-treating them; Roger shot at John Feukens, servant of William Croysere; being attached, they each made a fine for 40d.; pledges, Philip Erneys, John Bettelowe.

50. Benedictus Blundel[1] Willelmus Burcestre Iohannes Bundenho Walterus Picot Willelmus Freynshe Robertus Holewelle Robertus Tymcok Willelmus Kyng Iohannes atte March' Iohannes Ordwy Iohannes Bateman (et[i]) Iohannes Passewater dicunt per sacramentum suum quod Iohannes Tauntoft de Southyeuele in vigilia sancti Iohannis Baptiste anno regni regis Edwardi tercij vicesimo septimo apud Southyeuele verberauit et vulnerauit Oliuam Pik de eadem contra pacem. Qui quidem Iohannes attachiatus fuit ad respondendum domino regi et fecit finem et dat domino regi xiij s. iiij d. per plegium Willelmi Child et Roberti Lowys. (*Marg.* finem xiij s. iiij d.)

[1]Jury 9.

John Tauntoft of Southill, at Southill, beat and wounded Olive Pik of Southill; being attached, he made a fine for 13s. 4d.; pledges, William Child, Robert Lowys.

51. Dicunt eciam quod Robertus Gostwyk die Iouis proxima ante festum annunciacionis beate Marie anno regni regis Edwardi tercij post conquestum vicesimo tercio apud Wyliton' insultum fecit Galfrido Pecke de Stanford' et eum verberauit vulnerauit et male tractauit et super hoc idem Robertus eundem Galfridum ad certum locum vocatum Wyliton' bernes adduxit et ibidem eum imprisonauit quousque idem Galfridus eidem Roberto inuenerit plegios ad redempcionem faciendam ad voluntatem suam. Qui quidem Robertus attachiatus fuit ad respondendum domino regi et fecit finem et dat domino regi xx s. per plegium Benedicti Blundel et Rogeri Dunstale. (*Marg.* finem xx s.)

Robert Gostwyk, at Willington, assaulted Geoffrey Pecke of Stanford, beating, wounding, and maltreating him, and abducting him to Willington barn where he imprisoned him until Geoffrey gave pledges to pay a ransom; being attached, he made a fine for 20s.; pledges, Benedict Blundel, Roger Dunstale.

52. Dicunt eciam quod Robertus Gostwyk et Willelmus Godselawe frater dicti Roberti die Dominica proxima post festum natiuitatis beate Marie anno regni regis Edwardi tercij vicesimo quinto venerunt vi et armis in abbathiam de Wardon' et insultum fecerunt Waltero Hert de Wardon' et ipsum verberauerunt vulnerauerunt et male tractauerunt contra pacem per quod dictus Walterus iacuit in lecto suo per quartam partem anni proximo sequentis set dicunt quod indictati fuerunt coram Willelmo de Shareshull' et de hoc fecerunt finem. Qui quidem Robertus et Willelmus attachiati fuerunt ad respondendum domino regi et dictus Robertus fecit finem et dat domino regi vj s. viij d. per plegium Benedicti Blundel et Rogeri Dunstale et dictus Willelmus fecit finem et dat domino regi vj s. viij d. per plegium predictum. (*Marg.* finem vj s. viij d. finem vj s. viij d.)

Robert Gostwyk and his brother William Godselawe came armed to Warden abbey and assaulted Walter Hert of Warden, beating, wounding, and maltreating him; they were indicted before William de Shareshull and made fines; being attached, they each made a fine for 6s. 8d.; pledges, Benedict Blundel, Roger Dunstale.

For the summons of Robert before the King's Bench, Easter 1352, see K.B. 367, Rex, m. 38; 369, Rex, m. 68; for a fine by William, ibid., 367, Fines, m. 3.

53. Radulfus Beuchamp[1] Thomas Nicol Adam de Kent Iohannes Freynshe Iohannes Sneterlee Thomas Chil Robertus Pustel Willelmus

[1]Jury 10.

Laurence Iohannes de Wodhull' Willelmus Mustel Iohannes Scotteforde et Iohannes Letice dicunt per sacramentum suum quod die Lune proxima post festum natiuitatis beate Marie anno regni regis Edwardi tercij tricesimo apud Gritteford' Walterus Heruy holiwaterclerk de Sandeye Thomas Cartere Iohannes Auntrous et quidam extraneus insultum fecerunt Willelmo Golde de Gritteford noctanter et eum verberauerunt vulnerauerunt et male tractauerunt contra pacem. Qui quidem Walterus Thomas et Iohannes positi fuerunt in exigendis et per processum exacti fuerunt de comitatu in comitatum quousque vtlagati fuerunt. (*Marg.* vtlagati)

At Girtford Walter Hervy holy water clerk of Sandy, Thomas Cartere, John Auntrous, and a stranger assaulted William Golde of Girtford, beating, wounding, and maltreating him; they were exacted and outlawed.

54. Dicunt eciam quod Willelmus Leger de Estwyk' die Mercurij proxima post festum sancti Dionisij anno regni regis Edwardi tercij vicesimo nono apud Estwik' insultum fecit Alicie Top et eam verberauit contra pacem. Qui quidem Willelmus attachiatus fuit ad respondendum domino regi et fecit finem et dat domino regi iiij s. per plegium Benedicti Blundel et Hugonis Pikard. (*Marg.* finem iiij s.)

William Leger of Astwick, at Astwick, assaulted and beat Alice Top; being attached, he made a fine for 4s.; pledges, Benedict Blundel, Hugh Pikard.

[*m. 3*]
55. Radulfus Beuchamp[1] Thomas Nicol Adam de Ken Iohannes Freynshe Iohannes Sneterlee Thomas Child Robertus Pustel Willelmus Laurence Iohannes de Wodhull' Willelmus Mustel Iohannes Scotteford' et Iohannes Letice dicunt per sacramentum suum quod Iohannes persona ecclesie de Estwyk' die Lune proxima post festum sancti Michelis anno regni regis Edwardi tercij vicesimo nono apud Estwik' insultum fecit Alano Muleward et eum verberauit contra pacem. Qui quidem Iohannes attachiatus fuit ad respondendum domino regi et fecit finem et dat domino regi x s. per plegium Iohannis Harynger et Iohannis Pendel. (*Marg.* finem x s.)

John parson of Astwick, at Astwick, assaulted and beat Alan Muleward; being attached, he made a fine for 10s.; pledges, John Harynger, John Pendel.

56. Thomas Wrast[2] Iohannes de Salford Iohannes Porter Alexander Sherle Iohannes Sporoun Reginaldus Iurdan Iohannes Polayn Radulfus Clerk' Willelmus Fermory Iohannes Mile Willelmus Chalgraue et

[1]Jury 11.
[2]Jury 12.

Iohannes Northwode dicunt per sacramentum suum quod Iohannes le Peyntour de Euersholt fregit attachiamentum Walteri atte Chambre contra pacem qui quidem Walterus habuit perceptum Reginaldi de Grey iusticiarij domini regis ad ipsum attachiandum. Qui quidem Iohannes attachiatus fuit ad respondendum domino regi et fecit finem et dat domino regi x s. per plegium Iohannis Bekeryng chiualer et Walteri de Mershton'. (*Marg.* finem x s.)

John le Peyntour of Eversholt broke the arrest made by Walter atte Chambre on order of Reginald de Grey, justice of the king; being attached, he made a fine for 10s.; pledges, John Bekeryng, Kt., Walter de Mershton.
    See also below no. 76.

57. Dicunt eciam quod Adam capellanus et alij seruientes Alexandri Conditt de parochia de Birchemor ceperunt Iohannem Shepherde et ipsum detinuerunt contra voluntatem suam et contra pacem qui quidem Iohannes iuratus fuit ad seruiendum Iohanni Staleworthe cum idem Iohannes venerit ad domum dicti Alexandri pro panis suis habendis. Qui quidem Adam positus fuit in exigendis et per processum exactus de comitatu in comitatum quousque vtlagatus fuit. (*Marg.* vtlagatus)

Adam chaplain of Alexander Conditt of Birchmore and others of his servants detained John Shepherde who had sworn to serve John Staleworthe; Adam was exacted and outlawed.

58. Dicunt eciam quod Henricus Aldwynckle die Dominica proxima ante festum ramis palmarum anno regni regis Edwardi tercij tricesimo in campo de Woubourne in hundredo de Mannesheued felonice depredatus fuit Iohannem bercarium Iohannis de Morton' et ab eo felonice cepit vnam clokam procij xvj d. et vnum capicium precij xiiij d. et vj denarios dc pccunia numerata.

Henry Aldwynckle in the meadow of Woburn in Manshead hundred feloniously robbed John herdsman of John de Morton of a cloak, price 16d., a cap, price 14d., and 6d.
    See below no. 60.

59. Dicunt eciam quod idem Henricus die Iouis proxima ante festum ramis palmarum anno supradicto sub bosco de Woubourne felonice depredatus fuit Simonem le Smyth' de Tikeford' et de eo felonice cepit xj li. argenti et vnum equum precij xiij s. iiij d. et est communis latro.

The same Henry in the wood at Woburn feloniously robbed Simon le Smyth of Tickford [Berks] of £11 in silver and a horse, price 13s. 4d.; he is a common thief.
    See below no. 60.

60. Dicunt eciam quod idem Henricus die Lune proxima post festum epiphanie domini anno regni regis Edwardi tercij supradicto felonice furatus fuit vnum fardellum pannorum laneorum et lineorum et aliarum rerum precij v s. Qui quidem Henricus captus fuit et in prisona detentus quousque conuictus fuit coram Roberto de Throp'. (*Marg.* conuictus *bracketted to include nos. 58–60.*)

The same Henry feloniously stole a bundle of woollen and linen cloth and other goods, price 5s.; having been gaoled he was convicted before Robert de Throp.

Guilty, delivery Bedford gaol, 23 July 1356: pled clergy and released to ordinary for these three offences; G.D.R. 139, m. 5d.; 215/2, m. 224.

61. Willelmus Abbot[1] Ricardus le Clerk Thomas Bredon' Iohannes Grenewich' Iohannes atte Lane Iohannes Reynale Thomas Hikebit Robertus Hunwyne Rogerus Gillam Willelmus Beleuerge Willelmus Sampson et Philipus Totegos dicunt per sacramentum suum quod Willelmus Bocher de Seuelesho de die in diem minatur Willelmo Vmfrei ita quod non audet facere officium suum. Item dicunt quod idem Willelmus (Bocher[i]) die Martis proxima post festum sancti Iacobi anno regni regis Edwardi tercij vicesimo octauo vi et armis venit apud Maldon' et insultum fecit ibidem Ade le Taillour et ipsum verberauit contra pacem. Item dicunt quod idem Willelmus Bocher die Iouis proxima post festum sancte Margarete anno regni regis tercij supradicto venit apud Barton' et ibidem insultum fecit Iohanni Burnard et ipsum verberauit et vulnerauit contra pacem et est communis pungnator. Item dicunt quod idem Willelmus die Dominica proxima post festum inuencionis sancte crucis anno regni regis Edwardi tercij tricesimo apud Seuelesho minatus fuit Iohanni Friketo ad verberandum contra pacem. Qui quidem Willelmus positus fuit in exigendis et per processus exactus de comitatu in comitatum quousque vtlagatus fuit. (*Marg.* vtlagatus)

William Bocher of Silsoe daily threatened William Umfrei so that he dared not do his work; he assaulted and beat Adam le Taillour at Maulden; at Barton he assaulted John Burnard, beating and wounding him; he is a common fighter; at Silsoe he threatened to wound John Friketo; he was exacted and outlawed.

62. Dicunt eciam quod Edmundus Pulter de Cadyngdon' die Iouis proxima ante festum sancte Marie Magdalene anno regni regis Edwardi tercij vicesimo septimo apud Cadyngton' in communa Thome Bredon' insultum fecit bercario dicti Thome et ipsum verberauit contra pacem. Item dicunt quod idem Edmundus die Martis in vigilia sancti Iacobi apostoli anno supradicto venit vi et armis apud Cadyngdon' ad domum Thome de Bredon' et ibidem Iohannem Basset seruientem dicti Thome

[1] Jury 13.

cepit et abduxit contra pacem. Item dicunt quod idem Edmundus venit vi et armis apud Cadyngton' die et anno supradictis ad domum dicti Thome et in clausum dicti Thome intrauit et dictum Thomam de clauso suo fugauit contra pacem. Item dicunt quod idem Edmundus die Iouis proxima post festum sancti Petri aduincula anno regni regis Edwardi supradicto apud Luton' insultum fecit Willelmo Arderne de Luton' et ipsum verberauit contra pacem. Item dicunt quod idem Edmundus venit vi et armis die Iouis proxima post festum sancte Margarete anno regni regis Edwardi tercij vicesimo octauo apud Westcadyngdon' et cepit de Iohanne Carpenter de Westcadyngdon' x s. argenti et vnam bigam precij v s. et eum verberauit contra pacem. Item dicunt quod idem Edmundus die Sabati proxima post festum sancte Marie Magdalene anno regni regis Edwardi tercij tricesimo venit vi et armis apud Cadyngdon' et insultum fecit Micheli Pursele de Cadyngdon' et eum verberauit et vulnerauit contra pacem. Item dicunt quod idem Edmundus die Sabati in vigilia trinitatis anno regni regis Edwardi tercij tricesimo apud Estcadyngdon' insultum fecit Simoni Powel fratri hospitalis de Farleye et eum verberauit et sanguinem ab eo extraxit contra pacem. Item dicunt quod idem Edmundus die Sabati et anno supradictis apud Estcadyngdon' insultum fecit Iohanni Hyche seruienti magistri hospitalis de Farleye et eum verberauit et sanguinem ab eo extraxit contra pacem. Item dicunt quod idem Edmundus minatur magistro hospitalis predicti quod non audet morari in hospitali suo ideo petit remedium. .Qui quidem Edmundus positus fuit in exigendis et per processum exactus de comitatu in comitatum quousque vtlagatus fuit. Et postea recordum et processus vtlagarie predicte cum omnibus ea tangentibus coram domino rege mittuntur virtute cuiusdam breuis michi directi in hec verba.

Edwardus die gracia rex Anglie et Francie et dominus Hibernie dilecto et fideli suo Reginaldo de Grey salutem. Quia quibusdam certis de causis cerciorari volumus super recordo et processu vtlagarie in Edmundum Pulter de Cadyngdon' in comitatu Bed' promulgate et coram vobis et socijs vestris iusticiarijs nostris ad diuersas felonias et transgressiones in comitatu predicto audiendas et terminandas assignatis vt dicitur retornatis vobis mandamus quod recordum et processum vtlagarie predicte cum omnibus ea tangentibus nobis sub sigillo vestro distincte et aperte mittatis et hoc breue. Ita quod ea habeamus in octabis sancti Iohannis Baptiste vbicumque tunc fuerimus in Anglia vt vlterius inde fieri faciamus quod de iure et secundum legem et consuetudinem regni nostri Anglie fuerit faciendum. Teste me ipso apud Westm' xvj die Iunij anno regni regis nostri Anglie tricesimo primo [1357] regni vero nostri Francie decimo octauo. (*Marg.* coram rege per breue vtlagatus)

Edmund Pulter of Caddington, at Caddington, assaulted Thomas Bredon's herdsman on Thomas' common; he abducted John Basset, servant of Thomas

*Bredon from the latter's house; he drove Thomas out of his own close; at
Luton he assaulted William Arderne of Luton and beat him; at West
Caddington he took 10s. and a cart, price 5s., from John Carpenter and
beat him; at Caddington he assaulted Michel Pursele, beating and wounding
him; at East Caddington he assaulted brother Simon Powel of Farley
hospital, beating him and drawing blood; at East Caddington he assaulted
John Hyche servant of the master of Farley hospital, beating him and
drawing blood; he threatened the master of the hospital so that he dare not
remain in the hospital and so seeks remedy; Edmund was exacted and
outlawed. The record and process of the outlawry were sent to the King's
Bench on the following writ of* cerciorari *to Reginald de Grey.*

*Appeared before the King's Bench at Westminster, Trinity 1358; the
outlawry having been judged insufficient, he made a fine for 20s., for the
trespasses for which he was indicted; K.B. 388, Rex, m. 20; 392, Fines, m. 1.*

63. Dicunt eciam quod Iohannes le Soutere capellanus die Lune proxima
post festum natiuitatis sancti Iohannis Baptiste anno regni regis Edwardi
tercij tricesimo apud Flitte insultum fecit Thome Pichard et eum verberauit et vulnerauit contra pacem et est communis pugnator contra pacem.
Item dicunt quod idem Iohannes die et anno supradictis apud Flitte
insultum fecit Philipo Totegos et eum verberauit contra pacem. Qui
quidem Iohannes attachiatus fuit ad respondendum domino regi et fecit
finem et dat domino regi vj s. (viij d.[1]) per plegium Walteri Tiberd et
Willelmi Gurnard. (*Marg.* finem vj s. viij d.)

*John le Soutere chaplain, at Flitton, assaulted Thomas Pichard, beating and
wounding him; he is a common fighter; at Flitton he assaulted and beat
Philip Totegos; being attached, he made a fine for 6s. 8d.; pledges, Walter
Tiberd, William Gurnard.*

64. Iohannes Pertesoil[1] Ricardus Ledere Willelmus Iurdan Thomas
Mause Rogerus le Deen Iohannes Ichyngton' Willelmus Waukeleyn
Iohannes Reygner Iohannes le Eyr Robertus Gardiner Robertus Trate
et Willelmus Cole dicunt per sacramentum suum quod Willelmus
Bateman de Caysho die Dominica proxima post festum sancti Barnabe
apostoli anno regni regis Edwardi tercij vicesimo nono apud Caysho
fecit rescussum aueriorum Willelmo atte Ree seruienti magistri hospitalis
sancti Iohannis Bed' contra pacem domini regis. Qui quidem Willelmus
attachiatus fuit ad respondendum domino regi et fecit finem et dat
domino regi vj s. viij d. per plegium Rogeri Deen et Iohannis Raad.
(*Marg.* finem vj s. viij d.)

*William Bateman of Keysoe, at Keysoe, drove away cattle belonging to
William atte Ree servant of the master of the hospital of St John at*

[1] Jury 14.

Bedford; being attached, he made a fine for 6s. 8d.; pledges, Roger Deen, John Raad.

65. Dicunt eciam quod Adam Ace vicarius ecclesie de Oclee die Iouis in vigilia natiuitatis sancti Iohannis Baptiste anno regni regis Edwardi tercij tricesimo apud Oclee noctanter insultum fecit Agneti vxori Ade le Bere de Oclee et eam verberauit vulnerauit et brachium suum sinistrum in duobus locis fregit contra pacem. Qui quidem Adam attachiatus fuit ad respondendum domino regi et fecit finem et dat domino regi xl s. per plegium Willelmi Baxtere capellani et Iohannis Pikel. (*Marg.* finem xl s.)

Adam Ace vicar of Oakley, at Oakley, at night assaulted Agnes wife of Adam le Bere of Oakley, beating and wounding her, and breaking her left arm in two places; being attached, he made a fine for 40s.; pledges, William Baxtere chaplain, John Pikel.

66. Dicunt eciam quod Iohannes Pozoun de Caysho die Veneris proxima ante festum pentecostes anno regni regis Edwardi tercij tricesimo apud Caysho insultum fecit Henrico le Tailour de Caysho et eum verberauit contra pacem. Qui quidem Iohannes attachiatus fuit ad respondendum domino regi et fecit finem et dat domino regi xl d. per plegium Ricardi Ledere et Willelmi atte Graunge. (*Marg.* finem xl d.)

John Pozoun of Keysoe, at Keysoe, assaulted and beat Henry le Tailour of Keysoe; being attached, he made a fine for 40d.; pledges, Richard Ledere, William atte Graunge.

67. Dicunt eciam quod Iohannes filius Rogeri le Muleward de Caysho die Martis proxima ante festum epiphanie domini anno regni regis Edwardi tercij vicesimo nono apud Caysho insultum fecit Henrico Taillour de Caysho et eum verberauit contra pacem. Qui quidem Iohannes attachiatus fuit ad respondendum domino regi et fecit finem et dat domino regi x s. per plegium Willelmi atte Graunge et Willelmi Capicer. (*Marg.* finem x s.)

John son of Roger le Muleward of Keysoe, at Keysoe, assaulted and beat Henry Taillour of Keysoe; being attached, he made a fine for 10s.; pledges, William atte Graunge, William Capicer.

[*m. 3d.*]
68. Dicunt eciam quod Rogerus de Elyngton' Robertus garcio eiusdem Rogeri et Adam Carpenter capellanus die Sabati proxima post festum inuencionis sancte crucis anno regni regis Edwardi tercij tricesimo per assensum et procuracionem Iohannis de Holecote et Alianore vxoris sue apud Bolnhurst insultum fecerunt Iohanni le Eyr de Pertenhale et eum verberauerunt et vulnerauerunt contra pacem. Qui quidem Rogerus

Robertus Iohannes et Alianora attachiati fuerunt ad respondendum domino regi et dictus Rogerus fecit finem et dat domino regi ij s. per plegium Iohannis de Holecote de Pertenhale et dictus Robertus fecit finem et dat domino regi ij s. per plegium predictum et predicti Iohannes et Alianora fecerunt finem et dant domino regi vj s. viij d. per plegium Iohannis Astel et Rogeri Bippham et predictus Adam positus fuit in exigendis et per processum exactus de comitatu in comitatum quousque vtlagatus fuit. (*Marg.* finem ij s. finem ij s. finem vj s. viij d. vtlagatus)

Roger de Elyngton, his servant Robert, and Adam Carpenter chaplain with the assent and at the instigation of John de Holecote and his wife Eleanor, at Bolnhurst, assaulted John le Eyr of Pertenhall, beating and wounding him; being attached, Robert and Roger each made a fine for 2s., pledge, John de Holecote; John and Eleanor, for 6s. 8d.; pledges, John Astel, Roger Bippham; Adam was exacted and outlawed.

69. Dicunt eciam quod Simon Rogrom de Tilbrok die Sabati proxima ante festum sancti Petri aduincula anno regni regis Edwardi tercij vicesimo quarto apud Rislee ad domum Nicholai le Shepherde de Rislee et insultum ei fecit et de vita et membris ei minatur quousque dictus Nicholaus fecit finem cum eo et de eo cepit xiij s. iiij d. contra voluntatem suam et contra pacem domini regis. Qui quidem Simon attachiatus fuit ad respondendum domino regi et fecit finem et dat domino regi x s. per plegium Willelmi atte Graunge et Iohannis Ichyngton'. (*Marg.* finem x s.)

Simon Rogrom of Tilbrook, at Riseley, went to the house of Nicholas le Shepherde, assaulted him, and threatened him with death and injury until he made a fine for 13s. 4d.; being attached, Simon made a fine for 10s.; pledges, William atte Graunge, John Ichyngton.

70. Dicunt eciam quod Robertus Richard de Bolnhurst die Sabati proxima post festum inuencionis sancte crucis anno regni regis Edwardi tercij tricesimo apud Bolnhurst insultum fecit Iohanni Neweman de Colmorde et eum verberauit et vulnerauit contra pacem. Qui quidem Robertus attachiatus fuit ad respondendum domino regi et fecit finem et dat domino regi xij d. per plegium Iohannis Astel. (*Marg.* finem xij d.)

Robert Richard of Bolnhurst, at Bolnhurst, assaulted John Neweman of Colmworth, beating and wounding him; being attached, he made a fine for 12d.; pledge, John Astel.

71. Dicunt eciam quod Iohannes Payn de Therleye capellanus die Iouis proxima post festum translacionis sancti Thome martiris anno regni regis Edwardi tercij tricesimo apud Caysho insultum fecit Iohanni Welshe de Caysho et eum verberauit et male tractauit contra pacem. Qui quidem Iohannes attachiatus fuit ad respondendum domino regi et fecit finem et

5

dat domino regi vj s. viij d. per plegium Iohannis de la Leye et Roberti de Ipre. (*Marg.* finem vj s. viij d.)

John Payn of Thurleigh chaplain, at Keysoe, assaulted John Welshe of Keysoe, beating and maltreating him; being attached, he made a fine for 6s. 8d.; pledges, John de la Leye, Robert de Ipre.

72. Dicunt eciam quod Iohannes filius Roberti Erneys de Middulton' et Philipus Bordeleys die Lune proxima post festum natiuitatis domini anno regni regis Edwardi tercij vicesimo nono apud Middulton' insultum fecerunt Radulfo le Welshe seruienti Iohannis de Middulton' et eum verberauerunt contra pacem. Qui quidem Iohannes et Philipus attachiati fuerunt ad respondendum domino regi et dictus Iohannes fecit finem et dat domino regi xl d. per plegium Philipi Erneys et Iohannis fitz Iohan et dictus Philipus fecit finem et dat domino regi v s. per plegium Roberti Trate et Roberti Burdeleys. (*Marg.* finem xl d. finem v s.)

John son of Robert Erneys of Milton [Ernest] and Philip Bordeleys, at Milton, assaulted and beat Ralph le Welshe servant of John de Middulton; being attached, John made a fine for 40d.; pledges, Philip Erneys, John fitz Johan; Philip made a fine for 5s.; pledges, Robert Trate, Robert Burdeleys.

73. Willelmus Gurnard[1] Benedictus Blundel Willelmus Burcestre Robertus Holewelle Robertus Tymcok Willelmus Kyng Iohannes atte March' Thomas Adyngraue Radulfus atte Chambre Iohannes Bateman Adam Hoppere et Iohannes Passewater dicunt per sacramentum suum quod Bromine Robyn seruiens Walteri Tiberd die Mercurij proxima post festum apostolorum Philipi et Iacobi anno regni regis Edwardi tercij tricesimo apud Kerdyngton' insultum fecit Roberto Page et ipsum verberauit vulnerauit et male tractauit contra pacem. Et dictus Bromine Robin positus fuit in exigendis et per processum exactus de comitatu in comitatum quousque vtlagatus fuit. (*Marg.* vtlagatus)

Bromine Robyn servant of Walter Tiberd, at Cardington, assaulted Robert Page, beating, wounding, and maltreating him; he was exacted and outlawed.

74. Dicunt eciam quod Willelmus le Webbe de Coupol vulnerauit contra pacem domini regis Willelmum le Welshe et est communis perturbator pacis. Item dicunt quod idem Willelmus le Webbe sagittauit ex malicia precogitata Iohannem Passewater in pectore suo ita quod fuit in periculo mortis contra pacem. Qui quidem Willelmus attachiatus fuit ad respondendum domino regi et fecit finem et dat domino regi xx s. per plegium Iohannis Malynz et Rogeri Garkyn. (*Marg.* finem xx s.)

[1]Jury 15.

William le Webbe of Cople, a common disturber of the peace, wounded William le Welshe; with malice aforethought he shot John Passewater in the chest so that his life was in danger; being attached, he made a fine for 20s.; pledges, John Malynz, Roger Garkyn.

75. Iohannes Salford[1] Iohannes Sporoun de Herlyngdon' Henricus Hussebourne Iohannes Northwode Reginaldus Iurdan Iohannes Porter Alexander Shirlee Simon Loryng Iohannes de Morton' Robertus le Clerk de Woubourne Iohannes Polayn et Thomas Wrast dicunt per sacramentum suum quod Robertus Ouseflet persona ecclesie de Eueresholt die Martis proxima post festum sancti Gregorij anno regni regis Edwardi tercij tricesimo apud Eueresholt verberauit vulnerauit et male tractauit Iohannem Cholly de partibus borialibus contra pacem. Item dicunt quod die Iouis proxima post festum sancti Iacobi anno regni regis Edwardi tercij a conquestu tricesimo venit Walterus de la Chambre et Thomas Parker de Eton' cum commissione domini regis ad attachiandum Robertum personam ecclesie de Eueresholt in regia via de Eueresholt et predictus Robertus intellexit quod deberet attachiari statim fugit vsque rectoriam et tunc idem Robertus redijt de rectoria cum arcu et sagittis suis et felonice sagittauit dictum Thomam Parker cum sagitta supra genu per quam obijt. Item dicunt quod Reginaldus et Ricardus seruientes dicti Roberti venerunt contra pacem in auxilium dicti Roberti. Item dicunt quod die Iouis proxima post festum sancti Iacobi apostoli anno regni regis Edwardi tercij post conquestum tricesimo Walterus atte Chambre per commissionem domini regis venit in campo de Euersholt ad attachiandum malefactores et perturbatores pacis et ibi obuiauit cum Roberto rectore ecclesie de Euersholt sic dicendo dictus Walterus dixit dicto Roberto habeo tibi colloquium et ipse respondit quod nullum colloquium sibi vellet habere set statim se misit ad fugam vsque ad certum locum quo loco dictus Walterus sibi dixit quod habuit commissionem ipsum attachiare et ipse respondit quod venire deberet super periculum suum et traxit cultellum suum et alias se misit ad fugam vsque ad rectoriam suam de Euersholt. Et super hoc dictus Robertus inconcito [sic] Reginaldus et Ricardus seruientes sui venerunt extra rectoriam cum arcubus sagittis et baculis contra pacem domini regis in regia via de Euersholt et ibi obuiauerunt cum dicto Waltero et cum Thoma Parker de Eton' et ibi cum sagittis eorum dictis Waltero et Thoma sagittauerunt et dictum Thomam vulnerauerunt et male tractauerunt contra pacem domini regis ita quod de vita sua disperabatur et inconcito se miserunt in rectoriam et super hoc dictus Walterus et socij sui leuauerunt hutesium. Et postea omnia indictamenta dictum Robertum tangencia mittuntur in cancellariam domini regis virtute cuiusdam breuis michi directi in hec verba.

[1]Jury 16.

Edwardus dei gracia rex Anglie et Francie et dominus Hibernie dilecto et fideli suo Reginaldo de Grey de Ruthyn salutem. Cum nobis volentes omnia indictamenta facta coram vobis et socijs vestris iusticiarijs nostris ad diuersas felonias et transgressiones in comitatu Bed' audiendas et terminandas assignatis de quibuscumque felonijs et transgressionibus vnde Robertus persona ecclesie de Euersholt indictatus est vt dicitur coram nobis et non alibi terminari vobis mandamus sicut alias mandauimus quod omnia indictamenta predicta cum omnibus ea tangentibus qualitercumque vel per quodcumque nomen (in¹) indictamento predicto nominetur nobis in cancellariam nostram sub sigillo vestro distincte et aperte per aliquem de quo confiditis sine dilacione mittatis et hoc breue vel causam nobis significetis quare mandato nostro alias vobis inde directo minime paruistis. Teste me ipso apud Westm' xvj die Nouembris anno regni nostri Anglie tricesimo [1356] regni vero nostri Francie decimo septimo. (*Marg.* in cancellariam domini regis per breue)

Robert Ouseflet parson of Eversholt, at Eversholt, beat, wounded, and maltreated John Cholly. Walter de la Chambre and Thomas Parker of Eaton Ford, armed with a royal commission, came to arrest Robert but he fled to the rectory, armed himself with bows and arrows, and feloniously killed Thomas Parker. He was aided by his servants, Reginald and Richard. Walter and his companions raised the hue and cry. All indictments were sent to chancery on the following writ of mandamus *to Reginald de Grey.*

Isabel, widow of Thomas Shelford Parker of Eaton Ford, appealed Robert de Ouseflet parson of Eversholt, Thomas le Wright of Dunstable, and Robert atte Brok painter for the death of her husband in the King's Bench, Easter 1357; K.B. 387, Rex, m. 26d.; Michelmas 1357, made a fine for 1/2 mark for failure to proceed on the appeal; ibid., *389, Rex, m. 2d.; Fines, m. 3d.*

76. Dicunt eciam quod die Veneris proxima post quindenam pasche anno regni regis Edwardi tercij tricesimo Walterus atte Chambre per commissionem domini regis venit apud Euersholt et alij in societate sua ad domum Iohannis Peyntour et ipsum attachiauerunt per commissionem domini regis et statim dictum attachiatum fregit inconcito se misit ad fugam. Et dicunt quod dictus Iohannes Peyntour est perturbator pacis noctanter et de die in diem cum arcubus sagittis gladijs et alijs armis ita quod Radulfus Clerk et alij disperabantur de vita eorum. Qui quidem Iohannes attachiatus fuit ad respondendum domino regi et fecit finem et dat domino regi x s. per plegium Iohannis Bekeryng chiualer et Walteri de Mershton. (*Marg.* finem x s.)

Walter atte Chambre and others with a royal commission, at Eversholt, arrested John Peyntour who broke the arrest and fled; the said John is a disturber of the peace who goes about armed night and day so that Ralph

Clerk and others fear for their lives; being attached, John made a fine for 10s.; pledges, John Bekeryng, Kt., Walter de Mershton.
   See also above no. 56.

77. Dicunt eciam quod Hugo Meches de Hocleue die Mercurij proxima ante festum translacionis sancti Martini anno tricesimo verberauit vulnerauit et male tractauit Walterum Cornmongere de Badelusdon' in regia via de Hocleue contra pacem. Qui quidem Hugo attachiatus fuit ad respondendum domino regi et fecit finem et dat domino regi ij s. per plegium Iohannis Bekeryng chiualer et Nicholai persone ecclesie de Magna Brikhull'. (*Marg.* finem ij s.)

Hugh Meches of Hockliffe beat, wounded, and maltreated Walter Cornmongere of Battlesden on the king's highway in Hockliffe; being attached, he made a fine for 2s.; pledges, John Bekeryng, Kt., Nicholas parson of Great Brickhill.

[*m. 4*]
78. Robertus Carbommel[1] Walterus Picot Robertus Bele Walterus Gosefot Willelmus Cok Edmundus de Amundesham Ricardus Frereman Iohannes de Knottyng Thomas Spicer Willelmus Cleriuans Thomas Vigerous et Willelmus Litlee dicunt per sacramentum suum quod Rogerus Shethere de Bedeford' die Lune proxima post festum sancti Matthei apostoli anno regni regis Edwardi tercij tricesimo apud Bed' in presencia iusticiariorum domini regis tractauit cultellum suum Willelmo Prouisour contra pacem. Qui quidem Rogerus attachiatus fuit ad respondendum domino regi et fecit finem et dat domino regi v s. per plegium Iohannis de Knottyng et Thome Spicer. (*Marg.* finem v s.)

Roger Shethere of Bedford, at Bedford, on 26 September 1356, in the presence of the king's justices drew his knife on William Provisour; being attached, he made a fine for 5s.; pledges, John de Knottyng, Thomas Spicer.

79. Radulfus Beuchamp[2] Thomas Nicol Adam de Kent Iohannes Freynshe Iohannes Sneterlee Thomas Child Robertus Pustel Willelmus Laurence Iohannes de Wodhull' Willelmus Mustel Iohannes Scutteford' et Iohannes Letice dicunt per sacramentum suum quod die Martis proxima post festum translacionis sancti Thome martiris anno regni regis Edwardi tercij tricesimo apud Wrastlyngworthe Thomas Pye in clausum Iohannis Heruy de Wrastlyngworthe intrauit et ibidem prefato Iohanni et Agneti vxori sue vi et armis insultum fecit et illis minas imposuit de vita et membro gladio suo extracto contra pacem domini regis super quod

[1] Jury 17.
[2] Jury 18.

constabularij villate predicte venerunt et ex parte domini regis ei imper-
auerunt quod ad pacem domini regis plegios inuenerit qui quidem
Thomas secundum imperacionem constabulariorum predictorum se
iustificare noluit et super hoc idem Thomas est perturbator pacis domini
regis et de die in diem minas imponit Agneti vxori predicti Iohannis per
quas multum dubitat. Qui quidem Thomas positus fuit in exigendis et
per processum exactus de comitatu in comitatum quousque vtlagatus est.
(*Marg.* vtlagatus)

At Wrestlingworth Thomas Pye entered the close of John Hervy of
Wrestlingworth, assaulted the said John and his wife Agnes, and threatened
them with a drawn sword; the constables ordered Thomas to keep the peace
but he refused to take the oath; he is a disturber of the peace and continually
threatens Agnes; he was exacted and outlawed.

80. Dicunt eciam quod Simon le Muleward de Rokesdon' Ricardus le
Muleward de eadem et Rogerus Fullere de Caldecotemulne die Lune in
festo decollacionis sancti Iohannis Baptiste anno regni regis Edwardi
tercij tricesimo apud Bikeleswade insultum fecerunt Willelmo Coupere de
Rokesdon' et Willelmo Glouere de Sancti Iuone seruienti dicti Willelmi
Coupere et eos verberauerunt vulnerauerunt et male tractauerunt contra
pacem. Qui quidem Simon Ricardus et Rogerus attachiati fuerunt ad
respondendum domino (regi[1]) et dictus Simon fecit finem et dat domino
regi ij s. per plegium Willelmi de Holecote et Iohannis de Buddenho et
dictus Ricardus fecit finem et dat domino regi v s. per plegium predictum
et dictus Rogerus fecit finem et dat domino regi xl d. per plegium Rogeri
Garkyn et Ricardi Muleward. (*Marg.* finem ij s. finem v s. finem xl d.)

Simon le Muleward and Richard le Muleward both of Roxton and Roger
Fullere of Caldecote Mill, at Biggleswade, assaulted William Coupere of
Roxton and his servant William Glovere of St Ives [Hunts], beating,
wounding, and maltreating them; being attached, Simon made a fine for
2s., Richard, for 5s.; pledges, William de Holecote, John de Buddenho;
Roger made a fine for 40d.; pledges, Roger Garkyn, Richard Muleward.

81. Dicunt eciam quod Walterus le Daye de Langeforde die Iouis
proxima ante festum ramis palmarum anno regni regis Edwardi tercij
tricesimo noctanter intrauit domum Rosie Stowe et eam verberauit
contra pacem et eadem nocte idem Walterus verberauit Thomam Gemme
contra pacem. Qui quidem Walterus attachiatus fuit ad respondendum
domino regi et fecit finem et dat domino regi xiij s. iiij d. per plegium
Willelmi Freynshe et Ricardi Iuel. (*Marg.* finem xiij s. iiij d.)

Walter le Daye of Langford at night entered the house of Rose Stowe and
beat her; the same night he wounded Thomas Gemme; being attached, he
made a fine for 13s. 4d.; pledges, William Freynshe, Richard Ivel.

82. Dicunt eciam quod Henricus Holywaterclerk de Langeford die Veneris proxima post festum pasche anno regni regis Edwardi tercij tricesimo verberauit Aliciam de Esex contra pacem. Qui quidem Henricus attachiatus fuit ad respondendum domino regi et fecit finem et dat domino regi xiij s. iiij d. per plegium Willelmi de Holecote et Ricardi Iuel. (*Marg.* finem xiij s. iiij d.)

Henry Holywaterclerk of Langford beat Alice de Esex; being attached, he made a fine for 13s. 4d.; pledges, William de Holecote, Richard Ivel.

83. Dicunt eciam quod Iohannes Ioykyn de Rokesdon' et Iohannes Bate die Lune proxima post festum sancti Petri anno supradicto in villa de Bikeleswade verberauerunt Ricardum le Sawere de Caynho contra pacem. Qui quidem Iohannes et Iohannes attachiati fuerunt ad respondendum domino regi et dictus Iohannes Ioykyn fecit finem et dat domino regi vj s. viij d. per plegium Henrici de Bereford et Thome Bate et dictus Iohannes Bate dicit in nullo est culpabilis et de hoc ponit se super patriam. Ideo capiatur inde iurata que dicit quod in nullo est culpabilis. Ideo eat inde quietus. (*Marg.* finem vj s. viij d. quietus)

John Joykyn of Roxton and John Bate, at Biggleswade, beat Richard le Sawere of Keysoe; being attached, John Joykyn made a fine for 6s. 8d.; pledges, Henry de Bereford, Thomas Bate; John Bate pled not guilty and was acquitted.

84. Willelmus Fitz[1] Iohannes Cok Willelmus Seman Willelmus Maneby Ricardus Waryner Henricus Shelton' Iohannes Bromham Willelmus Pundere Iohannes Ballard Iohannes Haneto Robertus Hammes et Iohannes Welhul dicunt per sacramentum suum quod Henricus Pikard capellanus die Martis proxima post festum inuencionis sancte crucis anno regni regis Edwardi tercij tricesimo noctanter insultum fecit cuidam Waltero Rolfz seruienti suo et ipsum baculo verberauit vulnerauit et male tractauit contra pacem. Qui quidem Henricus attachiatus fuit ad respondendum domino regi et fecit finem et dat domino regi xij d. per plegium Iohannis Bretoun et Willelmi Fitz. (*Marg. finem* xij d.)

Henry Pikard chaplain at night assaulted his servant Walter Rolfz, beating him with a stick, wounding, and maltreating him; being attached, he made a fine for 12d.; pledges, John Bretoun, William Fitz.

85. Dicunt eciam quod Walterus Rolfz seruiens Henrici Pikard capellani die et anno supradictis dictum Henricum violenter et male vulnerauit et male tractauit contra pacem fere ad mortem. Qui quidem Walterus attachiatus fuit ad respondendum domino regi et fecit finem et dat domino regi vj s. viij d. per plegium Henrici magistri de Herdwyk' et Benedicti Blundel. (*Marg.* finem vj s. viij d.)

[1]Jury 19.

Walter Rolfz servant of Henry Pikard chaplain wounded the said Henry so badly that he nearly died; being attached, Walter made a fine for 6s. 8d.; pledges, Henry master of Hardwick, Benedict Blundel.

86. Dicunt eciam quod Iohannes Peuerel de Henlowe die Dominica in passione domini anno regni regis Edwardi tercij tricesimo apud Henlowe insultum fecit Rogero Taillour de Henlowe et ipsum verberauit vulnerauit et male tractauit contra pacem vi et armis. Qui quidem Iohannes attachiatus fuit ad respondendum domino regi et fecit finem et dat domino regi xx s. per plegium Willelmi Freynshe et Ricardi Steuenes. (*Marg.* finem xx s.)

John Peverel of Henlow, at Henlow, assaulted Roger Taillour of Henlow, beating, wounding, and maltreating him; being attached, he made a fine for 20s.; pledges, William Frenyshe, Richard Steuenes.

87. Dicunt eciam quod Iohannes le Smyth' de Magna Holewell' circa festum sancte Elene anno regni regis Edwardi tercij vicesimo quinto vi et armis et contra pacem insultum fecit Iohanni Fageswell de eadem et ibidem ipsum vulnerauit et male tractauit fere ad mortem et dictus Iohannes le Smyth' fugauit de patria ob causam quia indictatus fuit coram Shareshull' et nunc reuersus est ad patriam et manet cum Iohanne Druel et est communis malefactor. Qui quidem Iohannes le Smyth' attachiatus fuit ad respondendum domino regi et fecit finem et dat domino regi xiij s. iiij d. per plegium Iohannis Druel et Iohannis atte Stile. (*Marg.* finem xiij s. iiij d.)

John le Smyth of Holwell [Herts] assaulted John Fageswell of the same, wounding and maltreating him so that he nearly died; the said John le Smyth being indicted before [William] Shareshull fled the country; he has now returned and is living with John Druel; he is a common malefactor; being attached, he made a fine for 13s. 4d.; pledges, John Druel, John atte Stile.
For the indictment in the King's Bench see K.B. 367, Rex, m. 30d.; 368, Rex, m. 15; 370, Rex, m. 22.

88. Willelmus Abbot[1] Ricardus Clerk Thomas Bredon' Iohannes de Grenewich' Thomas Hikebid Rogerus Gilham Willelmus Sampsoun Philipus Totegos Ricardus de Faldo Willelmus Fullere Willelmus Botheby et Iohannes de Faldho dicunt per sacramentum suum quod Willelmus Worthyng et Adam Godday vagantes et faciunt contra pacem. Qui quidem Willelmus et Adam attachiati fuerunt ad respondendum domino regi et dictus Willelmus fecit finem et dat domino regi ij s. per plegium Henrici Skapelory et Ade Godday et dictus Adam fecit finem et dat

[1] Jury 20.

domino regi ij s. per plegium Iohannis Hicheman et Thome Hicheman. (*Marg.* finem ij s. finem ij s.)

William Worthyng and Adam Godday are vagrants and disturbers of the peace; being attached, they each made a fine for 2s.; pledges for William, Henry Skapelory, Adam Godday; for Adam, John Hicheman, Thomas Hicheman.

89. Dicunt eciam quod Iohannes Hicheman Thomas frater eius Willelmus Webbe et Iohannes Noteman vagantes et discurrunt armata contra pacem. Qui quidem Iohannes Thomas Willelmus et Iohannes attachiati fuerunt ad respondendum domino regi et dictus Iohannes Hicheman fecit finem et dat domino regi ij s. per plegium Iohannis Noteman et Ade Godday et dictus Thomas fecit finem et dat domino regi ij s. per plegium predictum et dictus Willelmus fecit finem et dat domino regi ij s. per plegium predictum et dictus Iohannes Noteman fecit finem et dat domino regi ij s. per plegium Iohannis Hicheman et Ade Godday. (*Marg.* finem ij s. finem ij s. finem ij s. finem ij s.)

John Hicheman, his brother Thomas, William Webbe, and John Noteman are vagrants who wander about armed; being attached, they each made a fine for 2s.; pledges, for John and Thomas Hicheman and William Webbe, John Noteman, Adam Godday; for John Noteman, John Hicheman, Adam Godday.

90. Dicunt eciam quod Iohannes atte Lane narrat consilium regis iusticiariorum et sociorum suorum. Qui quidem Iohannes attachiatus fuit ad respondendum domino regi de transgressione predicta qui dicit quod in nullo est culpabilis et de hoc ponit se super patriam. Ideo capiatur inde iurata que dicit quod in nullo est culpabilis. Ideo eat inde quietus. (*Marg.* quietus)

John atte Lane revealed the counsel of the king's justices; he pled not guilty and was acquitted.

91. Dicunt eciam quod Ricardus Worthyng' et Alexander Worthyng die Lune proxima ante festum pasche anno Edwardi tercij vicesimo nono venerunt vi et armis videlicet arcubus sagittis et gladijs in villa de Flitte et ibidem cuidam Ricardo Hake seruienti Thome prioris de Dunstapel piscanti in communi piscaria dicti prioris insultum fecerunt et ipsum verberauerunt vulnerauerunt et male tractauerunt et retia et alia ingenia dicti prioris ad valenciam xx s. ceperunt et asportauerunt contra pacem per quod dictus prior perdidit seruicium dicti Ricardi Hake per longum tempus. Qui quidem Ricardus Worthyng et Alexander attachiati fuerunt ad respondendum domino regi et dictus Ricardus fecit finem et dat domino regi xvj d. per plegium Willelmi Worthyng et Roberti Worthyng

et dictus Alexander fecit finem et dat domino regi xl d. per plegium predictum. (*Marg.* finem xvj d. finem xl d.)

Richard and Alexander Worthyng came armed to Flitton and there assaulted Richard Hake servant of the prior of Dunstable, who was fishing in the common fishpond; they beat, wounded, and maltreated him and carried away nets and other gear belonging to the prior valued at 20s.; thus the prior was deprived of Richard's service for a long time; being attached, they made fines, Richard for 16d., Alexander for 40d.; pledges, William Worthyng, Robert Worthyng.

[*m. 4d.*]

92. Dicunt eciam quod die Lune proxima post festum sancti Bartholomei anno regni regis Edwardi tercij tricesimo seruientes Thome prioris de Dunstapel ceperunt centum boues et vaccas facientes dampna in seperali dicti prioris in Flitwyk et eos in parco posuerunt et eodem die venerunt Iohannes Flemyng et Ricardus Worthyng vi et armis videlicet arcubus sagittis et baculis et predictas bestias a seruientibus dicti prioris ceperunt et abduxerunt et bestias dicti prioris sagittauerunt et predictos seruientes vsque in manerium de Rokeshokes fugauerunt ita quod non ausi fuerunt extra manerium predictum ire ad faciendum officium suum per longum tempus contra pacem domini regis. Qui quidem Ricardus attachiatus fuit ad respondendum domino regi et fecit finem et dat domino regi ij s. per plegium Willelmi Worthyng et Roberti Worthyng et dictus Iohannes positus fuit in exigendis et per processum exactus de comitatu in comitatum quousque vtlagatus fuit. (*Marg.* finem ij s. vltagatus)

After the servants of Thomas, prior of Dunstable, had branded 100 oxen and put them in the prior's park at Flitwick, John Flemyng and Richard Worthyng armed with bows, arrows, and sticks, drove away the cattle and injured them; the servants, having fled to the manor of Ruxox were afraid to leave it to perform their duties; being attached, Richard made a fine for 2s.; pledges, William Worthyng, Robert Worthyng; John was exacted and outlawed.

93. Martinus le Eyr[1] Iohannes le Sweyn Ricardus Northwode Thomas Stepynglee Thomas Richer Iohannes atte Hokes Willelmus Comquest Iohannes de Mershton' Willelmus Doget Iohannes Lillyngston Willelmus Richer Robertus Deystere Ricardus Tiuyle et Iohannes ofthe Moor dicunt per sacramentum suum quod die Mercurij proxima post festum sancti Laurencij anno regni regis Edwardi tercij tricesimo apud Ampthull' Rogerus filius Rogeri le Wariner de Ampthull' felonice furatus fuit lx s. de pecunia numerata de Philipo le Spicer de Ampthull' et est communis latro. Qui quidem Rogerus captus fuit et in prisona detentus quousque

[1]Jury 21.

deliberatus fuit apud Dunstapel coram Willelmo de Notton'. (*Marg.* coram W de Notton')

At Ampthill Roger son of Roger le Wariner of Ampthill feloniously stole 60s. from Philip le Spicer of Ampthill; he is a common thief; he was freed from Dunstable gaol by William de Notton.

Indicted before the King's Bench at Dunstable, Michelmas 1357, for this and other offences; judged guilty; pled clergy and released to the ordinary; K.B. 389, Rex, m. 25d.; this same term Peter de Salford, former sheriff of Bedfordshire was fined 100s. because Wariner escaped while in the sheriff's custody; ibid., Fines, m. 2.

94. Dicunt eciam quod Thomas Iargeuille de Maldon' die Lune proxima post festum sancti Benedicti anno regni regis Edwardi tercij tricesimo apud Maldon' insultum fecit Iohanni Neel de Maldon' et ipsum verberauit vulnerauit et adhuc multas minas ei imponit de vita et membro contra pacem. Qui quidem Thomas attachiatus fuit ad respondendum domino regi et fecit finem et dat domino regi vj s. viij d. per plegium Iohannis atte Hokes et Walteri Pikard. (*Marg.* finem vj s. viij d.)

Thomas Jargeville of Maulden, at Maulden, assaulted John Neel of Maulden, beating, wounding, and threatening his life; being attached, he made a fine for 6s. 8d.; pledges, John atte Hokes, Walter Pikard.

95. Iohannes Pertesoil[1] Ricardus Ledere Willelmus Waukeleyn Thomas Mause Willelmus Betheree Iohannes Ichyngton' Willelmus Bateman Rogerus Bispham Galfridus Michel Iohannes Bolle Willelmus Oyldeboef' et Iohannes Kyng dicunt per sacramentum suum quod die Sabati proxima post festum sancti Bartholomei apostoli anno regni regis Edwardi tercij tricesimo apud le Hoo in Tilbrok Iohannes Redeswelle del Hoo felonice interfecit Ricardum le Skynnere del Hoo et ab eo ibidem cepit et felonice asportauit c s. de pecunia numerata. Et postea istud indictamentum mittitur coram rege virtute cuiusdam breuis michi inde directi in hec verba.

Edwardus dei gracia rex Anglie et Francie et dominus Hibernie dilecto et fideli suo Reginaldo de Grey salutem. Quia Iohannes de Redeswelle qui in prisona marescalcie nostre coram nobis certis de causis detinetur coram vobis et socijs vestris iusticiarijs nostris ad diuersas felonias et transgressiones in comitatu Bed' audiendas et terminandas assignatis de diuersis felonijs vt accepimus est indictatus vobis mandamus sicut pluries vobis mandauimus quod omnia indictamenta ipsum Iohannem qualitercumque tangencia et penes vos residencia sub sigillo vestro distincte et aperte mittatis coram nobis in octabis purificacionis beate Marie vbicumque tunc fuerimus in Anglia vt vlterius inde fieri faciamus quod secundum

[1]Jury 22.

legem et consuetudinem regni nostri Anglie inde fore viderimus faciendum vel causam nobis significetis quare mandata nostra tociens vobis inde directa exequi noluisti vel non potuistis et habeatis ibi hoc breue. Teste W de Shareshull' apud Westm' xxvj die Ianuarij anno regni nostri Anglie tricesimo primo [1357] regni nostri Francie decimo octauo. (*Marg.* coram rege per breue)

At the Hoo in Tilbrook [Hunts] John Redeswelle of the Hoo feloniously killed Richard le Skynnere of the Hoo and robbed him of 100s.; the indictment is sent to the King's Bench on the following writ of mandamus *to Reginald de Grey.*

After two writs of mandamus, *this one and one of the previous 20 October 1356, John Redeswelle, in the bishop of London's prison at Stortwell, was brought before the King's Bench, found guilty, and sentenced to be hanged, Trinity 1357; K.B. 385, Rex, m. 25; see also* ibid., *387, Rex, m. 27.*

96. Henricus Blaunkfrount[1] Iohannes Salford' Iohannes Porter Iohannes Morton' Reginaldus Iurdon Thomas Lynleye Henricus Hussebourne Radulfus Clerk Henricus Skapelory Iohannes de Northwode Robertus le Clerk de Woubourne et Iohannes de Mulsho dicunt per sacramentum suum quod Gilbertus Coleman de Woubournechapel die Lune in festo apostolorum Philipi et Iacobi anno regni regis tercij tricesimo primo apud Woubournechapel in domum Willelmi Peshoun de Woubournechapel intrauit et insultum ei fecit et eum verberauit vulnerauit et male tractauit contra pacem. Qui quidem Gilbertus attachiatus fuit ad respondendum domino regi et fecit finem et dat domino regi xiij s. iiij d. per plegium Reginaldi Iurdon et Radulfi le Clerk'. (*Marg.* finem xiij s. iiij d.)

Gilbert Coleman of Woburn Chapel, at Woburn Chapel, entered the house of William Peshoun of Woburn Chapel and assaulted him, beating, wounding, and maltreating him; being attached, he made a fine for 13s. 4d.; pledges, Reginald Jurdon, Ralph le Clerk.

97. Willelmus Fitz[2] Iohannes Cok Willelmus Seman Willelmus Maneby Ricardus Waryner Henricus Shelton' Iohannes Bromham Willelmus Peendere Iohannes Ballard Iohannes Haneto Robertus Hammes et Iohannes Wellehul dicunt per sacramentum suum quod Elias le Muleward de Stotfeld' die Sabati in vigilia sancti Iacobi anno regni regis Edwardi tercij post conquestum tricesimo apud Stotfeld insultum fecit Alicie Daye de eadem et eam verberauit et male tractauit contra pacem. Qui quidem Elias attachiatus fuit ad respondendum domino regi et fecit finem et dat domino regi vj s. viij d. per plegium Willelmi Saman et Ade Chanceler. (*Marg,* finem vj s. viij d.)

[1] Jury 23.
[2] Jury 24.

Elias le Muleward of Stotfold, at Stotfold, assaulted Alice Daye of Stotfold, beating and maltreating her; being attached, he made a fine for 6s. 8d.; pledges, William Saman, Adam Chanceler.

98. Dicunt eciam quod Iuliana Britteuille die Martis proxima post festum sancti Iohannis ante portam latinam anno regni regis Edwardi tercij tricesimo primo apud Dunstapel insultum fecit Agneti vxori Iohannis Wirkman de Houghton' Regis et eam verberauit et male tractauit contra pacem. Que quidem Iuliana attachiata fuit ad respondendum domino regi et fecit finem et dat domino regi vj d. per plegium Willelmi Haddon' et Ricardi Albon. (*Marg.* finem vj d.)

Juliana Britteville, at Dunstable, assaulted Agnes wife of John Wirkman of Houghton Regis, beating and maltreating her; being attached, she made a fine for 6d.; pledges, William Haddon, Richard Albon.

99. Iohannes de Kent[1] Adam de Kent Willelmus Mustel Iohannes de Wodhull' Thomas Nichol Iohannes de Bramhton' Iohannes Letice Willelmus Laurence Iohannes le Freynshe Thomas Child Galfridus Hanuylle et Willelmus Richeman dicunt per sacramentum suum quod Ricardus le Sawere de Campton' die Lune proxima post festum sancte Marie Magdalene anno regni regis Edwardi tercij tricesimo apud Bikeleswade insultum fecit Iohanni Tarpot de Campton' et ipsum verberauit vulnerauit et male tractauit contra pacem. Item dicunt quod idem Ricardus circa festum natiuitatis sancti Iohannis Baptiste anno regni regis Edwardi tercij tricesimo apud Camelton' insultum fecit Willelmo Couherde et ipsum ibidem vulnerauit et male tractauit contra pacem et est communis verberator. Qui quidem Ricardus attachiatus fuit ad respondendum domino regi et fecit finem et dat domino regi xxvj s. viij d. per plegium Nicholai Meperteshale et Iohannis Muleward. (*Marg.* finem xxvj s. viij d.)

Richard le Sawere of Campton, at Campton, assaulted John Tarpot of Campton, beating, wounding, and maltreating him; likewise at Campton he assaulted William Couherde, wounding and maltreating him; he is a common beater; being attached, he made a fine for 26s. 8d.; pledges, Nicholas Meperteshale, John Muleward.

100. Dicunt eciam quod Hugo de Welles de Kerbrok' Willelmus Wareyner de Neketon' et Ricardus Wilde capellanus die Veneris proxima post festum sancti Matthei apostoli anno regni regis Edwardi tercij post conquestum tricesimo apud Grittefordebrigge noctanter depredauerunt

[1]Jury 25.

Stephanum Robyn de Wauyngdon' de vno equo precij xx s. et de vno male de diuersis coloribus cum bonis in eadem precij x s. et de xxiiij s. argenti de pecunia numerata et ibidem dictum Stephanum felonice interfecerunt et hoc per assensum et abettum fratris Iohannis de Hawle fratris hospitalis sancti Iohannis de Ierusalem in Anglie et fratris Iohannis Neuyle fratris eiusdem hospitalis. Qui quidem Hugo Willelmus Ricardus Iohannes et Iohannes positi fuerunt in exigendis et per processum exacti de comitatu in comitatum quousque vtlagati fuerunt. (*Marg.* vtlagati)

Hugh de Welles of Carbrooke [Norf], William Wareyner of Necton [Norf], and Richard Wilde chaplain, at Girtford Bridge, at night robbed Stephan Robyn of Wavendon [Bucks], of a horse, price 20s., a multicoloured bag and contents, price 10s., and 24s. in cash, and then feloniously killed him; this they did with the assent and aid of John de Hawle and John Nevyle brothers of the hospital of St John of Jerusalem in England; all five were exacted and outlawed.

101. Dicunt eciam quod Adam Ielyon die Dominica proxima ante festum pentecostes anno regni regis nunc tricesimo primo verberauit Thomam Clerk' contra pacem. Qui quidem Adam attachiatus fuit ad respondendum domino regi et fecit finem et dat domino regi xl d. per plegium Iohannis Bailly et Ricardi le Smyth'. (*Marg.* finem xl d.)

Adam Jelyon beat Thomas Clerk; being attached, he made a fine for 40d.; pledges, John Bailly, Richard le Smyth.

102. Dicunt eciam quod Iohannes Bate de Rokesdon' die Lune proxima post festum sancti Nicholai anno regni regis Edwardi tercij vicesimo nono apud Bikeleswade insultum fecit Nicholao Auncel et ipsum verberauit imprisonauit et detinuit quousque idem Nicholaus fecit ei finem de xl d. contra pacem. Qui quidem Iohannes attachiatus fuit ad respondendum domino regi et fecit finem et dat domino regi x s. per plegium Henrici de Bereford et Thome Bate. (*Marg.* finem x s.)

John de Bate of Roxton, at Biggleswade, assaulted and beat Nicholas Auncel and imprisoned him until he made a fine for 40d.; being attached, John made a fine for 10s.; pledges, Henry de Bereford, Thomas Bate.

[*m. 5*]
103. Iohannes de Buddenho[1] Willelmus Boynoun Walterus Picot Willelmus Freynshe Willelmus Gurnard Willelmus Kyng Iohannes Passewater Iohannes Bateman Nicholaus Pecke Willelmus Clement Iohannes atte March' et Radulfus atte Chambre dicunt per sacramentum
[1]Jury 26.

suum quod Iohannes Dogges de Elnestowe die Lune proxima post festum annunciacionis beate Marie anno regni regis Edwardi tercij tricesimo primo apud Elnestowe felonice furatus fuit vnum iumentum precij vj s. viij d. de Willelmo Belu. Qui quidem Iohannes captus fuit et in prisona detentus quousque deliberatus fuit coram Roberto de Thorp.' Ideo eat inde quietus. (*Marg.* coram Roberto de Thorp')

John Dogges of Elstow, at Elstow, feloniously stole a mare, price 6s. 8d., from William Belu; being delivered from gaol by William de Thorp, he was acquitted.

Acquitted, delivery of Bedford gaol, 21 July 1357; G.D.R. 216/1, m. 96.

104. Iohannes Pertesoil[1] Iohannes Cole de Rislee Willelmus Waukeleyn Ricardus Ledere Willelmus Bateman Iohannes Rolt Iohannes Bailly Iohannes Bolle Willelmus Cole de Rislee Willelmus Oyldeboef' de Pertenhale Willelmus Bethe Ree et Robertus Haycroft dicunt per sacramentum suum quod Thomas Rolt de Rauenesden' et Thomas Rolt filius eiusdem Thome venerunt die Sabati proxima post festum inuencionis sancte crucis anno regni regis nunc tricesimo primo apud Rauenesden' cum gladijs fustibus et armis et insultum fecerunt Iohanni Astel de Bolnhurst et ipsum verberauerunt vulnerauerunt et male tractauerunt contra pacem. Qui quidem Thomas et Thomas attachiati fuerunt ad respondendum domino regi et dictus Thomas Rolt fecit finem et dat domino regi vj s. viij d. per plegium Iohannis Reed et Iohannis Pippard et dictus Thomas filius eius fecit finem et dat domino regi vj s. viij d. per plegium predictum. (*Marg.* finem vj s. viij d. finem vj s. viij d.)

Thomas Rolt of Ravensden and his son Thomas, at Ravensden, being armed assaulted John Astel of Ravensden, beating, wounding, and maltreating him; being attached, each made a fine for 6s. 8d.; pledges, John Reed, John Pippard.

105. Willelmus Abbot[2] Ricardus de Faldho Ricardus Clerk' Henricus Messager Iohannes Bradysan Thomas Bredon' Iohannes Wilcous Iohannes atte Lane Iohannes Laulee iunior Iohannes Grenewych' Iohannes Aungeuyn et Hugo atte Welle dicunt per sacramentum suum quod Iohannes Greneford' de Luton' die Dominica proxima post festum decollacionis sancti Iohannis ·anno regni regis nunc tricesimo apud Luton' insultum fecit Sabine Camstere et eam verberauit contra pacem. Qui quidem Iohannes attachiatus fuit ad respondendum domino regi et fecit finem et dat domino regi v s. per plegium Roberti Bere et Iohannis Adde. (*Marg.* finem v s.)

[1]Jury 27.
[2]Jury 28.

John Greneford of Luton, at Luton, assaulted Sabina Camstere and beat her; being attached, he made a fine for 5s.; pledges, Robert Bere, John Adde.

106. Dicunt eciam quod die Dominica post festum natiuitatis beate Marie anno regni regis Edwardi tricesimo apud Luton' Iohannes Durant de Luton' insultum fecit Nicholao Cartere et eum verberauit et vulnerauit contra pacem. Qui quidem Iohannes attachiatus fuit ad respondendum domino regi et fecit finem et dat domino regi x s. per plegium Arnoldi Soutere et Hamonis le Clerk'. (*Marg.* finem x s.)

At Luton John Durant of Luton assaulted Nicholas Cartere, beating and wounding him; being attached, he made a fine for 10s.; pledges, Arnold Soutere, Hamo le Clerk.

107. Dicunt eciam quod Willelmus Cartere de Luton' die Dominica proxima ante festum pentecostes anno regni regis nunc tricesimo apud Luton' insultum fecit Iohanni Wilkyn et eum verberauit contra pacem. Qui quidem Willelmus attachiatus fuit ad respondendum domino regi et fecit finem et dat domino regi vj s viij d. per plegium Iohannis Adde et Arnoldi Soutere. (*Marg.* finem vj s. viij d.)

William Cartere of Luton, at Luton, assaulted and beat John Wilkyn; being attached, he made a fine for 6s. 8d.; pledges, John Adde, Arnold Soutere.

108. Dicunt eciam quod Adam Broun de Luton' die Dominica proxima post festum sancti Laurencij anno regni regis nunc tricesimo apud Luton' insultum fecit Waltero seruienti Roberti Saleman et eum verberauit contra pacem. Qui quidem Adam attachiatus fuit ad respondendum domino regi et fecit finem et dat domino regi vj s. viij d. per plegium Iohannis atte Park' et Hamonis le Clerk'. (*Marg.* finem vj s. viij d.)

Adam Broun of Luton, at Luton, assaulted and beat Walter servant of Robert Saleman; being attached, he made a fine for 6s. 8d.; pledges, John atte Park, Hamo le Clerk.

109. Dicunt eciam quod Robertus Benehale de Mogerhanger die Sabati proxima post festum sancte Marie Magdalene anno regni regis Edwardi tercij tricesimo apud Seuelesho venit vi et armis et insultum fecit Iohanni Sampson de Seuelesho et eum verberauit vulnerauit et male tractauit contra pacem ita quod de vita sua disperabatur. Qui quidem Robertus attachiatus fuit ad respondendum domino regi et fecit finem et dat domino regi v s. per plegium Iohannis Malynz et Radulfi atte Chambre. (*Marg.* finem v s.)

Robert Benehale de Mogerhanger, at Silsoe, assaulted John Sampson of Silsoe, beating, wounding, and maltreating him so that his life was in danger; being attached, he made a fine for 5s.; pledges, John Malynz, Ralph atte Chambre.

110. Dicunt eciam quod Ricardus Beuere (de Flamstede[1]) die Veneris proxima ante festum sancte trinitatis anno regni regis nunc tricesimo primo apud Markyate venit vi et armis et insultum fecit Willelmo Cok de Luton' et eum verberauit contra pacem et est communis malefactor. Qui quidem Ricardus attachiatus fuit ad respondendum domino regi et fecit finem et dat domino regi xl d. per plegium Willelmi de Woubourne et Iohannis Bekeryng chiualer. (*Marg.* finem xl d.)

Richard Bevere of Flamstead [Herts], at Markyate [Herts], assaulted and beat William Cok of Luton; he is a common malefactor; being attached, he made a fine for 40d.; pledges, William de Woubourne, John Bekeryng, Kt.

111. Iohannes de la Leye[1] Willelmus Mordant senior Iohannes de Stoke Iohannes Heruy Robertus de Wodhull' Iohannes le Whyte Thomas le Bray Iohannes Bramham Robertus Edward Iohannes Pollescroft Ricardus Stockere et Iohannes Balteswelle dicunt per sacramentum suum quod Petrus de Bolnho die Lune proxima ante festum Dominice ramis palmarum anno regni regis nunc tricesimo primo apud Blecuesho insultum fecit Thome Bole constabulario et seruienti domini regis et ipsum verberauit in domo predicti Thome contra pacem. Qui quidem Petrus attachiatus fuit ad respondendum domino regi et fecit finem et dat domino regi vj s. viij d. per plegium Iohannis Pertesoil et Iohannis Alsey. (*Marg.* finem vj s. viij d.)

Peter de Bolnho, at Bletsoe, assaulted and beat Thomas Bole constable and king's servant, in the latter's house; being attached, he made a fine for 6s. 8d.; pledges, John Pertesoil, John Alsey.

112. Henricus de Bereford[2] Robertus Lord Ricardus Englys Thomas Baa Thomas Saltere Walterus Veyse Iohannes Chanu Iohannes Golde de Diuelho Thomas Broun Simon Lache Iohannes le Beer et Euerardus Agu dicunt per sacramentum suum quod Radulfus Berde de Wilden' die Sabati proxima post festum inuencionis sancte crucis anno regni regis Edwardi tercij tricesimo primo apud Wilden' insultum fecit Iohanni Craomfeld et eum verberauit et fregit policem dicti Iohannis contra pacem. Qui quidem Radulfus attachiatus fuit ad respondendum domino regi et fecit finem et dat domino regi xl d. per plegium Ricardi Englys et Walteri Taillour. (*Marg.* finem xl d.)

Ralph Berde of Wilden, at Wilden, assaulted John Croamfeld, beating him and breaking his thumb; being attached, he made a fine for 40d.; pledges, Richard Englys, Walter Taillour.

[1]Jury 29.
[2]Jury 30.

6

113. Dicunt eciam quod Nicholaus Picot de Ronhale die Iouis proxima ante festum sancti Martini anno regni regis Edwardi tercij tricesimo apud Wilden' venit vi et armis noctanter et ibidem insultum fecit Ricardo Englys de Wilden' et eum verberauit vulnerauit et male tractauit contra pacem ita quod de vita sua disperabatur et hoc fecit quia idem Ricardus iuratus fuit in seruicio domini regis. Qui quidem Nicholaus attachiatus fuit ad respondendum domino regi et fecit finem et dat domino regi xiij s. iiij d. per plegium Willelmi Picot et Iohannis Astel. (*Marg.* finem xiij s. iiij d.)

Nicholas Picot of Renhold, at Wilden, at night assaulted Richard Englys of Wilden, beating, wounding, and maltreating him so that his life was in danger; this Nicholas did because Richard was a juror in the king's service; being attached, he made a fine for 13s. 4d.; pledges, William Picot, John Astel.

114. Dicunt eciam quod Willelmus Quarel de Bereford die Veneris in septimana pentecostes anno regni regis Edwardi tercij tricesimo primo apud Bereford insultum fecit Iohanni Freysheryng baxtere et eum verberauit et vulnerauit contra pacem. Qui quidem Willelmus attachiatus fuit ad respondendum domino regi et fecit finem et dat domino regi viij s. per plegium Iohannis le Erl senioris et Iohannis Cote. (*Marg.* finem viij s.)

William Quarel of Barford, at [Great] Barford, assaulted John Freysheryng baker, beating and wounding him; being attached, he made a fine for 8s.; pledges, John le Erl, sr., John Cote.

115. Willelmus Saman[1] Iohannes Bretoun Willelmus in the Mede Willelmus Fitz Iohannes Cok' Adam Chaunceler Iohannes le Man Iohannes Maysemor Galfridus Frankeswclle Willelmus Laurence Willelmus Maneby et Adam Laurence dicunt per sacramentum suum quod Iohannes filius Hamonis le Clerk de Eyen circa festum natiuitatis sancti Iohannis Baptiste anno regni regis Edwardi tercij tricesimo apud Shutlyngdon' insultum fecit Iohanni atte Wode constabulario domini regis et ibidem ipsum verberauit vulnerauit et male tractauit contra pacem et est communis verberator. Qui quidem Iohannes filius Hamonis attachiatus fuit ad respondendum domino regi et fecit finem et dat domino regi v s. per plegium Hamonis le Clerk et Galfridi Broun. (*Marg.* finem v s.)

John son of Hamo le Clerk of Ion, at Shillington, assaulted John atte Wode, king's constable, beating, wounding, and maltreating him; this he commonly does; being attached, he made a fine for 5s.; pledges, Hamo le Clerk, Geoffrey Broun.

[1]Jury 31.

116. Dicunt eciam quod Willelmus Thorpele est communis verberator contra pacem. Qui quidem Willelmus attachiatus fuit ad respondendum domino regi et fecit finem et dat domino regi xl d. per plegium Iohannis Cok et Iohannis Sparwe. (*Marg.* finem xl d.)

William Thorpele is a common flogger; being attached, he made a fine for 40d.; pledges, John Cok, John Sparwe.

117. Dicunt eciam quod Gilbertus le Rous de Shefford die Veneris proxima post festum sancti Matthei apostoli anno regni regis Edwardi tercij tricesimo primo apud Shefford insultum fecit Roberto Boteler et Thome Pope constabularijs domini regis et eos verberauit et male tractauit contra pacem quia ipsi constabularij fecerunt officium suum. Qui quidem Gilbertus attachiatus fuit ad respondendum domino regi et fecit finem et dat domino regi x s. per plegium Rogeri le Yonge et Simonis Betoun. (*Marg.* finem x s.)

Gilbert le Rous of Shefford, at Shefford, assaulted Robert Boteler and Thomas Pope, king's constables, because they were functioning in their office; being attached, he made a fine for 10s.; pledges, Roger le Yonge, Simon Betoun.

118. Robertus Carbommel[1] Henricus Shareman Robertus Bele Hugo Lauche Thomas Spicer Walterus Gosefot Willelmus Crowe Iohannes Daubour Iohannes Knottyng Adam Yerdelee Willelmus Rauenesdon' et Iohannes Forster dicunt per sacramentum suum quod Rogerus Mayn de Bedeford et Iuliana vxor eius venerunt vi et armis die Veneris proxima post festum sancti Petri aduincula anno regni regis Edwardi tercij tricesimo primo apud Bed' et insultum fecerunt Iohanne Holle de Bedeford et ipsam verberauerunt vulnerauerunt et male tractauerunt contra pacem. Qui quidem Rogerus et Iuliana attachiati fuerunt ad respondendum domino regi et fecerunt finem et dant domino regi x s. per plegium Thome de Eston' et Iohannis Frereman. (*Marg.* finem x s.)

Roger Mayn of Bedford and his wife Juliana, at Bedford, assaulted Johanna Holle of Bedford, beating, wounding, and maltreating her; being attached, they made a fine for 10s.; pledges ,Thomas de Eston, John Frereman.

119. Dicunt eciam quod Rogerus le Shethere venit cum hominibus ignotis vi et armis die Veneris proxima post festum sancti Petri aduincula anno regni regis Edwardi tercij tricesimo primo ad domum Rogeri Mayn in Bedeford et ibidem eidem Rogero Mayn insultum fecit cum scuto et cultello tracto ita quod dictus Rogerus Mayn non ausus fuit domum suam exire set imparcatus fuit contra pacem. Qui quidem Rogerus le

[1]Jury 32.

Shethere attachiatus fuit ad respondendum (domino regi[i]) de transgressione predicta qui dicit quod in nullo est culpabilis et de hoc ponit se
super patriam. Ideo capiatur inde iurata que dicit quod in nullo est
culpabilis. Ideo eat inde quietus. (*Marg.* quietus)

Roger le Shethere with unknown men came to the house of Roger Mayn in
Bedford and assaulted him with a sword and a drawn knife; Roger Mayn
did not dare leave his house; being attached, Roger le Shethere pled not
guilty; the jury acquitted him.

120. Thomas Beuerelee[1] Iohannes Pertesoil Iohannes le Heir Robertus
Haycroft Iohannes Bolle Willelmus Wysman Iohannes Saundres Walterus
le Eyr Rogerus Byspham Simon Pertesoil Walterus Vmfrei et Willelmus
Masoun dicunt per sacramentum suum quod Adam vicarius ecclesie de
Oclee die Iouis in festo corporis Christi anno regni regis Edwardi tercij
tricesimo primo apud Oclee insultum fecit Edwardo clerico et seruienti
dicti Ade et ipsum verberauit vulnerauit et male tractauit contra pacem.
Qui quidem Adam attachiatus fuit ad respondendum domino regi et
fecit finem et dat domino regi vj s. viij d. per plegium Roberti Fysshere
et Iohannis Marchal. (*Marg.* finem vj s. viij d.)

Adam vicar of Oakley, at Oakley, assaulted Edward, a clerk who was his
servant, beating, wounding, and maltreating him; being attached, he made
a fine for 6s. 8d.; pledges, Robert Fysshere, John Marchal.

[*m. 5d.*]
121. Dicunt eciam quod Thomas Dodeman de Rislee et Willelmus
Aylbern die Lune proxima ante festum sancti Michelis anno regni regis
Edwardi tercij tricesimo primo noctanter apud Rislee felonice fregerunt
domum Iohannis Pertesoil et ibidem felonice furati fuerunt vnum manu-
tergium vnam mappam et vnam maceram precij xx s. et vnum equum
et vnam sellam cum freno precij xx s. de predicto Iohanne. Qui quidem
Thomas et Willelmus capti fuerunt et in prisona detenti quousque
deliberati fuerunt apud Dunstapel coram Willelmo de Notton.' (*Marg.*
coram W de Notton')

Thomas Dodeman of Riseley and William Aylbern, at Riseley, at night
feloniously broke into the house of John Pertesoil and feloniously stole a
towel, a napkin, and a bowl, price 20s., and a horse and a saddle with a
bridle, price 20s.; they were freed from gaol at Dunstable by William de
Notton.

   Both, on indictment before the justices of the peace, brought before the
King's Bench delivering Bedford gaol at Dunstable, Michelmas 1357;
acquitted; K.B. 389, Rex, m. 31.

[1]Jury 33.

122. Iohannes de Kent[1] Adam de Kent Willelmus Mustel Iohannes de Wodhull' Thomas Nichol Iohannes de Bramhton' Iohannes Letice Willelmus Laurence Iohannes Freynshe Thomas Child Galfridus Haunuylle Willelmus Richeman et Iohannes Stutteford dicunt per sacramentum suum quod Willelmus le Clerk seruiens persone ecclesie de Temesford die Iouis in festo exaltacionis sancte crucis anno regni regis Edwardi tercij tricesimo primo apud Temesford insultum fecit Roberto Pustel et ipsum secutus fuit cum cultello tracto ita quod de vita sua disperabatur et ipsi minatur de die in diem ita quod non audeat per vias ire contra pacem. Qui quidem Willelmus attachiatus fuit ad respondendum domino (regi[1]) et fecit finem et dat domino regi v s. per plegium Willelmi de Holecote et Iohannis de Middilton. (*Marg.* finem v s.)

William le Clerk servant of the parson of Tempsford, at Tempsford, assaulted Robert Pustel, pursuing him with a drawn knife so that his life was endangered; he daily threatened Robert so that the latter did not dare go on the highway; being attached, he made a fine for 5s.; pledges, William de Holecote, John de Middilton.

123. Dicunt eciam quod Willelmus persona ecclesie de Temesford est manutentor dicti Willelmi Clerk' in facto predicto contra pacem et in alijs similibus. Qui quidem Willelmus persona attachiatus fuit ad respondendum domino regi et fecit finem et dat domino regi v s. per plegium Willelmi de Holecote et Iohannis de Middilton. (*Marg.* finem v s.)

William parson of Tempsford supported William Clerk in the aforesaid deed as he has in others like it; being attached, he made a fine for 5s.; pledges, William de Holecote, John de Middilton.

124. Benedictus Blundel[2] Iohannes de Buddenho Walterus Picot Willelmus Boynoun Willelmus Freynshe Willelmus Gurnard Iohannes Passewater Nicholaus Pecke Iohannes Ordwy Willelmus Kyng Willelmus Clement et Radulfus atte Chambre dicunt per sacramentum suum quod Adam Blakebourne die Dominica proxima post festum sancti Matthei apostoli anno regni regis Edwardi tercij tricesimo primo apud Gekewelle insultum fecit Roberto Wodehewere et ipsum verberauit vulnerauit et male tractauit contra pacem. Qui quidem Adam attachiatus fuit ad respondendum domino regi et fecit finem et dat domino regi x s. per plegium Thome le Scok et Roberti Wolmongere. (*Marg.* finem x s.)

Adam Blakebourne, at Ickwell, assaulted Robert Wodehewere, beating, wounding, and maltreating him; being attached, he made a fine for 10s.; pledges, Thomas le Scok, Robert Wolmongere.

[1]Jury 34.
[2]Jury 35.

125. Dicunt eciam quod Nicholaus Taillour de Caldecote die Sabati in vigilia pentecostes anno regni regis Edwardi tercij tricesimo primo apud Caldecote insultum fecit Rogero Garkyn balliuo domini regis et Agneti vxori eius et eos verberauit vulnerauit et male tractauit contra pacem. Qui quidem Nicholaus attachiatus fuit ad respondendum domino regi et fecit finem et dat domino regi ij s. per plegium Roberti Doucessone et Iohannis Parkere. (*Marg.* finem ij s.)

Nicholas Taillour of Caldecote, at Caldecote, assaulted Roger Garkyn, king's bailiff, and his wife Agnes, beating, wounding, and maltreating them; being attached, he made a fine for 2s.; pledges, Robert Doucessone, John Parkere.

126. Dicunt eciam quod Willelmus seruiens domine Matillis de Trumpeton' die Martis proxima post festum omnium sanctorum anno regni regis Edwardi tercij vicesimo nono apud Mogerhanger insultum fecit Iohanni Southe et ipsum verberauit vulnerauit et male tractauit contra pacem. Qui quidem Willelmus attachiatus fuit ad respondendum domino regi et fecit finem et dat domino regi xl d. per plegium Roberti Tymcok et Henrici Vmfrei. (*Marg.* finem xl d.)

William servant of Lady Matilda de Trumpeton, at Mogerhanger, assaulted John Southe, beating, wounding, and maltreating him; being attached, he made a fine for 40d.; pledges, Robert Tymcok, Henry Umfrei.

127. Dicunt eciam quod Iohannes Becke nuper balliuus persone ecclesie de Blounham die Dominica proxima post festum sancti Matthei apostoli anno regni regis Edwardi tercij tricesimo primo apud Southmulne noctanter insultum fecit Rogero Munde soutere et ipsum verberauit vulnerauit et male tractauit contra pacem et est communis malefactor. Qui quidem Iohannes attachiatus fuit ad respondendum domino regi et fecit finem et dat domino regi x s. per plegium Willelmi atte Hoo et Iohannis Caldewelle. (*Marg.* finem x s.)

John Becke, former bailiff of the parson of Blunham, at South Mills, at night assaulted Roger Munde, cobbler, beating, wounding, and maltreating him; he is a common malefactor; being attached, he made a fine for 10s.; pledges, William atte Hoo, John Caldewelle.

128. Thomas Spicer[1] Willelmus Rauenesden' Adam Bisshop Thomas Peyntour Robertus Bele Iohannes Forster Willelmus Cok Walterus Fysshere Thomas Vigerous Nicholaus in the Lane Iohannes le Cook' et Hugo le Smyth' dicunt per sacramentum suum quod Walterus le Soutere qui disponsauit vxorem quondam Thome Duston' Hugo Werkman et Iohannes Maldon' soutere die Lune in festo circumcisionis domini anno

[1]Jury 36.

regni regis Edwardi tricesimo primo apud Bedeford noctanter se lati-
tauerunt in abscondito et insultum fecerunt Iohanni Correyour et cuidam
extraneo et ipsos verberauerunt et male vulnerauerunt et male tractauerunt contra pacem. Et dicunt quod idem Walterus communiter se latitat
in abscondito noctanter ad verberandum homines et est communis
verberator et malefactor contra pacem. Qui quidem Walterus Hugo et
Iohannes attachiati fuerunt ad respondendum domino regi et dictus
Walterus fecit finem et dat domino regi xiij s. iiij d. per plegium Radulfi
Lote et Iohannis Donne et dictus Hugo fecit finem et dat domino regi
vj s. viij d. per plegium Hugonis Lauche et Iohannis Frereman et dictus
Iohannes fecit finem et dat domino regi vj s. viij d. per plegium predictum.
(*Marg.* finem xiij s. iiij d. finem vj s. viij d. finem vj s. viij d.)

Walter le Soutere, betrothed to the wife of the late Thomas Duston, Hugh
Werkman, and John Maldon, cobbler, at Bedford, at night concealed
themselves and assaulted John Correyour and a stranger, beating, badly
wounding, and maltreating them; Walter commonly lurks at night to beat
people and is a common beater and malefactor; being attached, Walter
made a fine for 13s. 4d.; pledges, Ralph Lote, John Donne; Hugh and John
for 6s. 8d. each; pledges, Hugh Lauche, John Frereman.

129. Benedictus Blundel[1] Iohannes Buddenho Walter Picot Willelmus
Boynoun Willelmus Freynshe Willelmus Gurnard Iohannes Passewater
Nicholaus Pecke Iohannes Ordwy Willelmus Kyng Willelmus Clement
et Radulfus atte Chambre dicunt per sacramentum suum quod Willelmus
filius Willelmi Tele de Keryngton' noctanter insultum fecit Thome
Malherbe et ipsum verberauit vulnerauit et male tractauit contra pacem.
Qui quidem Willelmus attachiatus fuit ad respondendum domino regi et
fecit finem et dat domino regi xl d. per plegium Willelmi Boynoun et
Rogeri Garkyn. (*Marg.* finem xl d.)

William son of William Tele of Cardington at night assaulted Thomas
Malherbe, beating, wounding, and maltreating him; being attached, he
made a fine for 40d.; pledges, William Boynoun, Roger Garkyn.

130. Dicunt eciam quod Willelmus Muleward de Temesford narrauit
consilium domini regis et sociorum suorum. Qui quidem Willelmus
attachiatus fuit ad respondendum domino regi et fecit finem et dat
domino regi xl d. per plegium Hugonis le Bray et Hugonis le Rede.
(*Marg.* finem xl d.)

William Muleward of Tempsford revealed the counsel of the king and of
his fellows; being attached, he made a fine for 40d.; pledges, Hugh le Bray,
Hugh le Rede.

[1]Jury 37.

131. Martinus le Eyr[1] Willelmus Pynnok Willelmus ofthe Felde Robertus Wodhull' Thomas atte Rode Thomas Southwode Radulfus Catelyn Willelmus Godwyne Willelmus Terry Laurencius Seintjohan Robertus Burgeys Laurencius Sidekyn et Walterus Ridelere dicunt per sacramentum suum quod Willelmus Grymesby manens apud Berton' die Sabati in festo assumpcionis beate Marie anno regni regis Edwardi tercij vicesimo nono apud Crannfeld felonice furatus fuit quemdam equum Thome Southwode precij vj s. viij d. Item dicunt quod idem Willelmus die Veneris proxima ante festum natiuitatis beate Marie anno supradicto apud Crannfeld felonice furatus fuit quemdam equum Radulfi Catelyne precij x s. Qui quidem (Willelmus[i]) positus fuit in exigendis et per processum exactus de comitatu in comitatum quousque vtlagatus fuit. Item dicunt quod idem Willelmus die Lune proxima ante festum omnium sanctorum anno supradicto apud Crannfeld felonice furatus fuit quemdam equum precij v s. Simone Barton' et est communis Iatro. Qui quidem Willelmus vtlagatus fuit vt supra. (*Marg.* vtlagatus)

William Grymesby living in Barton, at Cranfield, feloniously stole a horse, price 6s. 8d., from Thomas Southwode, a horse, price 10s., from Ralph Catelyne, a horse, price 5s,. from Simon Barton; he is a common thief; he was exacted and outlawed.

132. Dicunt eciam quod Thomas Burray de Elnestowe et Willelmus Taillour quondam seruiens Iohannis Phelpot de Elnestowe sunt vagantes de die in diem et de nocte in noctem et habent in awayt Iohannem Beydon' et ipsi manifeste minantur de vita et membris contra pacem. Qui quidem Thomas et Willelmus attachiati fuerunt ad respondendum domino regi et dictus Thomas fecit finem et dat domino regi xl d. per plegium Walteri de Mershton' et Iohannis de Shelton' et dictus Willelmus fecit finem et dat domino regi xl d. per plegium predictum. (*Marg.* finem xl d. finem xl d.)

Thomas Burray of Elstow and William Taillour former servant of John Phelpot of Elstow are vagrants night and day; they waylaid John Beydon and threatened him with injury to life and limb; being attached, they each made a fine for 40d.; pledges, Walter de Mershton, John de Shelton.

133. Ricardus Ledere[2] Iohannes Parker Willelmus Bateman Iohannes Keselyngbury Simon Waryner Iohannes Reyner Robertus Haycroft Willelmus Masoun Robertus Gardiner Robertus Cook' Iohannes Molle et Iohannes Saundre dicunt per sacramentum suum quod Robertus Pikeman de London' et Thomas Fynch' de Baldok die Sabati proxima post festum sancti Gregorij anno regni regis Edwardi tercij tricesimo

[1]Jury 38.
[2]Jury 39.

secundo vi et armis clausum Willelmi Tapicer apud Stoghton' paruam fregerunt et in Agnetem vxorem dicti Willelmi ibidem insultum fecerunt et ipsam verberauerunt vulnerauerunt et male tractauerunt contra pacem. Qui quidem Robertus et Thomas positi fuerunt in exigendis et per processum exacti de comitatu in comitatem quousque vtlagati fuerunt. (*Marg.* vtlagati)

Robert Pikeman of London and Thomas Fynch of Baldock [Herts] broke into the close of William Tapicer at Little Staughton and assaulted William's wife Agnes, beating, wounding, and maltreating her; they were exacted and outlawed.

[*m.* 6]

134. Iohannes Bolle[1] Willelmus Bethere Willelmus Wysman Iohannes West Iohannes Nicous Michel Smyth' Willelmus Reymer Willelmus Baillif Henricus Muleward Willelmus Fauceloun Walter le Eyr et Ricardus de Tyssyngton' dicunt per sacramentum suum quod Simon Harleys de Rislee venit die sancti Laurencij anno regni regis Edwardi tercij vicesimo octauo apud Knottyng et ibidem depredauit duos equos precij xx s. felonice de Ricardo de Tissyngton' clerico. Item quod idem Simon venit die sancti Martini anno supradicto apud Knottyng' ibidem felonice depredauit vnum equum precij xiij s. iiij d. de predicto Ricardo. Item dicunt quod idem Simon die purificacionis beate Marie virginis anno regni regis Edwardi tercij tricesimo secundo venit apud le Temple ad domum Iohannis Hert et domum suam ibidem felonice fregit et lyntheamina tapetes et superlectula et alia bona et catalla dicti Iohannis ad valenciam xxx s. ibidem inuenta felonice furatus fuit. Item dicunt quod idem Simon prima die Dominica xlme anno regni regis Edwardi tercij tricesimo secundo venit apud Yeuelden' ad domum Willelmi Croyser et ibidem felonice furatus fuit iiij^{or} lyntheamina ij tapetes j cooperlectulum j tunicam cum capicio et j par caligarum precij in toto vj s. viij d. de duobus garcionibus dicti Willelmi. Item dicunt quod idem Simon die Martis proxima post medium xlme anno regni regis Edwardi tercij tricesimo secundo venit apud Knottyng cum alijs latronibus ignotis et ecclesiam ibidem felonice fregit et vnam pixidem cum reliquibus precij c s. ibidem inuentum furatus fuit. Qui quidem Simon captus fuit et in prisone detentus quousque deliberatus fuit coram Roberto de Thorp' et Iohanne Knyuet. Ideo eat (inde[i]) quietus. (*Marg.* coram R de Thorp')

Simon Harleys of Riseley, at Knotting, feloniously stole two horses, price 20s., and one horse, price 13s. 4d., from Richard de Tissyngton clerk; at Templewood, he feloniously broke into the house of John Hert and feloniously stole sheets, carpets, coverlets, and other goods valued at 30s.; at

[1] Jury 40.

Yelden from William Croyser's house he feloniously stole four sheets, two carpets, a coverlet, a tunic with a hood, and a pair of gloves, price in toto *6s. 8d., from two servants; at Knotting, with other unknown thieves he feloniously broke into the church and stole a pix with relics, price 100s.; he was liberated from gaol by Robert de Thorp and John Knyvet and acquitted.*

Acquitted, delivery Bedford gaol, 12 September 1358; G.D.R. 215/2, m. 72; see also ibid., *m. 60, 20 July 1359; he was indicted before Reginald de Grey.*

135. Dicunt eciam quod Thomas Waryn manens cum Galfrido de Drayton' die Iouis proxima ante festum sancti Gregorij anno regni regis Edwardi tercij tricesimo secundo apud Stoghton' paruam venit vi et armis noctanter et insultum fecit Iohanni Muryman et ipsum verberauit vulnerauit et digitum dicti Iohannis amputauit contra pacem. Item dicunt quod idem Thomas illud fecit per assensum procuracionem et abettum Willelmi de Grantesden' et Iohanne vxoris eius. Qui quidem Thomas Willelmus et Iohanna attachiati fuerunt ad respondendum domini regi et dictus Thomas fecit finem et dat domino regi x s. per plegium Willelmi Grantesden' et Dauid Bailli et dicti Willelmus et Iohanna fecerunt finem et dant domino regi vj s. viij d. per plegium Iohannis Astel et Iohannis de Goldyngton. (*Marg.* finem x s. finem vj s. viij d.)

Thomas Waryn living with Geoffrey de Drayton, at Little Staughton, at night assaulted John Muryman, beating and wounding him, and cutting off a finger; he did this at the instigation and with the aid of William de Grantesden and his wife Johanna; being attached, the three made fines, Thomas for 10s.; pledges, William Grantesden, David Bailli; William and Johanna for 6s. 8d.; pledges, John Astel, John de Goldyngton.

136. Dicunt eciam quod Thomas Clopton' de parua Stoghton' die Iouis proxima ante festum sancti Gregorij anno regni regis Edwardi tercij tricesimo secundo apud Rauenesden' insultum fecit Iohanni Raad et ipsum verberauit et vulnerauit contra pacem. Qui quidem Thomas attachiatus fuit ad respondendum domino regi et fecit finem et dat domino regi vj s. viij d. per plegium Walteri le Eyr et Iohannis Wolf. (*Marg.* finem vj s. viij d.)

Thomas Clopton of Little Staughton, at Ravensden, assaulted John Raad, beating and wounding him; being attached, he made a fine for 6s. 8d.; pledges, Walter le Eyr, John Wolf.

137. Dicunt eciam quod Iohannes Pulter de Therleye die Lune proxima ante festum sancti Marcij anno regni regis Edwardi tercij tricesimo secundo apud Therleye felonice furatus fuit tres oues precij v s. de

Iohanne Hayward et tres oues precij v s. de Willelmo atte Hacche. Et dicunt quod Robertus Aunfleys et Robertus Soor receptauerunt predictas oues apud Caysho scientes feloniam predictam et predicti Robertus et Robertus tres oues vendiderunt apud Kynebauton' die Lune in festo sancti Georgij anno supradicto et tres oues vendiderunt ad villam Sancti Neoti die Iouis proxima ante festum sancti Georgij anno supradicto vt manutentores felonie predicte. Item dicunt quod Robertus Aunfleys receptauit ad domum suam propriam in Caysho bona et catalla dicti Iohannis Pulter noctanter postquam iste Iohannes fugauit patriam propter feloniam predictam et illa bona elongauit in adiuuacionem ipsius Iohannis. Qui quidem Iohannes positus fuit in exigendis et per processum exactus de comitatu in comitatem quousque vtlagatus fuit. Et predicti Robertus et Robertus capti fuerunt et in prisona detenti quousque deliberati fuerunt coram Roberto de Thorp' et Iohanne Knyuet. Ideo eant inde quieti. (*Marg.* vtlagatus quieti)

John Pulter of Thurleigh, at Thurleigh, feloniously stole three sheep, price 5s., from John Hayward and three sheep, price 5s., from William atte Hacche; Robert Aunfleys and Robert Soor received the sheep at Keysoe knowing they were stolen; they sold three at Kimbolton [Hunts] and three at St Neots [Hunts]; Robert Aunfleys received at his house in Keysoe goods and chattels of the said John after the latter had fled the country because of the aforesaid felony; John was exacted and outlawed; the others were released from gaol by Robert de Thorp and John Knyvet and acquitted.

Robert Aunfleys and Robert Soor, on indictment before John Marshall and John Rokesdon, acquitted, delivery Bedford gaol, 12 September 1358; G.D.R. 215/2, m. 71.

138. Iohannes Kent[1] Adam Kent Thomas Child Iohannes Bramhton' Iohannes Letice Robertus Pustel Willelmus Laurence Iohannes Scutteford Iohannes Muriel Willelmus Brokende Iohannes Nowesle et Ricardus Steuenes dicunt per sacramentum suum quod Rogerus seruiens Iohannis de Raston' et Willelmus Braunch' seruiens dicti Iohannis die Martis proxima post festum annunciacionis beate Marie anno regni regis nunc tricesimo secundo apud Wrastlyngworthe fecerunt rescussum Willelmo Simondessone balliuo Iohannis Malyng' vnius collectoris x^e et xvme et constabulario villate de Wrastlyngworthe venienti cum dicto balliuo videlicet de vno equo capto pro porcione xvme dicti Iohannis de Raston' videlicet iij s. contra pacem. Qui quidem Rogerus et Willelmus positi fuerunt in exigendis et per processum exacti de comitatu in comitatem quousque vtlagati fuerunt. (*Marg.* vtlagati)

Roger and William Braunch servants of John de Raston, at Wrestlingworth, took from William Simondessone, bailiff of John Malyng, collector of the

[1]Jury 41.

10th and 15th, and constable of Wrestlingworth, a horse given in part payment of the 15th by John de Raston, i.e., 3s.; they were exacted and outlawed.

139. Dicunt eciam quod Iohannes Godknaue de Saundeye die Sabati in vigilia pasche anno regni regis nunc tricesimo secundo apud Saundeye fecit rescussum Rogero Aubrey balliuo dicti Iohannis Malyng de vno boue capta pro xv^{ma} et ipsum verberauit contra pacem. Qui quidem Iohannes attachiatus fuit ad respondendum domino regi et fecit finem et dat domino regi ij s. per plegium Roberti Tymcok et Willelmi atte Hoo. (*Marg.* finem ij s.)

John Godknave of Sandy, at Sandy, took from Roger Aubrey, bailiff of the same John Malyng, an ox given in payment of the 15th and wounded him; being attached, he made a fine for 2s.; pledges, Robert Tymcok, William atte Hoo.

140. Robertus de Hammes[1] Rogerus le Cook Ricardus Dauy Henricus filius Walteri Willelmus Muleward Thomas Smyth' Iohannes de Dalton' Iohannes Blanncoft Nicholaus atte Welle Iohannes Clergys Radulfus Litlee et Iohannes atte Moor de Radewelle dicunt per sacramentum suum quod Iohannes le Smyth' de Felmersham die Lune proxima post festum sancti Marcij anno regni regis nunc tricesimo secundo apud Felmersham insultum fecit Thome le Sook balliuo domini regis et cultellum suum et ensem tractauit et ipsum extra villam fugauit contra pacem et est communis malefactor. Qui quidem Iohannes attachiatus fuit ad respondendum domino regi et fecit finem et dat domino regi xx s. per plegium Willelmi Bynde et Willelmi Yep. (*Marg.* finem xx s.)

John le Smyth of Felmersham, at Felmersham, assaulted Thomas le Sook, king's bailiff, drew his knife and sword, and drove Sook from the village; he is a common malefactor; being attached, he made a fine for 20s.; pledges, William Bynde, William Yep.

141. Benedictus Blundel[2] Robertus Tymcok Iohannes Buddenho Walterus Picot Willelmus Burcestre Robertus Holewelle Thomas Adyngraue Willelmus Kyng Iohannes atte March' Willelmus Freynshe Henricus Vmfrey Willelmus Craas et Nicolaus Pecke dicunt per sacramentum suum quod Petrus Caperoun de Wendeye die Sabati in vigilia penetcostes anno regni regis Edwardi tercij tricesimo secundo apud Fenlake insultum fecit Agneti vxori Willelmi de Siresham et ipsam verberauit contra pacem. Qui quidem (Petrus[i]) attachiatus fuit ad respondendum domino regi et fecit finem et dat domino regi xij d. per plegium Iohannis Mareschal et Ricardus Crannfeld. (*Marg.* finem xij d.)

[1]Jury 42.
[2]Jury 43.

Peter Caperoun of Wendy [Cambs], at Fenlake, assaulted and beat Agnes wife of William de Siresham; being attached, he made a fine for 12d.; pledges, John Mareschal, Richard Crannfeld.

142. Dicunt eciam quod Iohannes de Kempston' die Lune in crastino pentecostes anno supradicto apud Fenlake insultum fecit Iohanni Boynoun et ipsum verberauit et vulnerauit contra pacem et Willelmus Cok fuit auxilians et consenciens prefato Iohanni de Kempston' ad verberacionem predictam. Qui quidem Iohannes de Kempston' et Willelmus attachiati fuerunt ad respondendum domino regi et dictus Iohannes fecit finem et dat domino regi x s. per plegium Willelmi Waryner et Iohannis Appelee et dictus Willelmus fecit finem et dat domino regi xl d. per plegium predictum. (*Marg.* finem x s. finem xl d.)

John de Kempston, at Fenlake, assaulted John Boyoun, beating and wounding him; he was aided by William Cok; being attached, they made fines, John for 10s., William for 40d.; pledges, William Waryner, John Appelee.

143. Henricus de Bereford[1] Iohannes Blundel Thomas Saltere Walterus Len Veyse Robertus Lord Iohannes Chanu Elias Smyth' Thomas Baa Henricus Pippard Iohannes fitz Hugth' Thomas Broun et Iohannes Stockere dicunt per sacramentum suum quod Iohannes Haye de Bolnhurst et Iohannes Ropere de Ford iunior sunt communes malefactores contra pacem. Qui quidem Iohannes et Iohannes attachiati fuerunt ad respondendum domino regi et dictus Iohannes Haye fecit finem et dat domino regi ij s. per plegium Iohannis Astel et Walteri Dekene et dictus Iohannes Ropere fecit finem et dat domino regi xl d. per plegium Iohannis Batesford et Walteri Auncel. (*Marg.* finem ij s. finem xl d.)

John Haye of Bolnhurst and John Ropere, jr., of Eaton Ford, are common malefactors; being attached, they made fines, John Haye for 2s.; pledges, John Astel, Walter Dekene; John Ropere, jr., for 40d.; pledges, John Batesford, Walter Auncel.

144. Dicunt eciam quod Willelmus Persoun de Stapulho et Stephanus Golde de eadem sunt communes malefactores contra pacem. Qui quidem Willelmus et Stephanus attachiati fuerunt ad respondendum domino regi et dictus Willelmus fecit finem et dat domino regi v s. per plegium Willelmi Oliuer et Iohannis Elys et dictus Stephanus fecit finem et dat domino regi ij s. per plegium Walteri Pollard et Iohannis Pollard. (*Marg.* finem v s. finem ij s.)

William Persoun and Stephan Golde, both of Staploe, are common malefactors; being attached, they made fines, William for 5s.; pledges, William Oliver, John Elys; Stephan for 2s.; pledges, Walter Pollard, John Pollard.

[1]Jury 44.

[*m. 6d.*]

145. Thomas Child[1] Thomas Nichol Willelmus Mustel Willelmus Laurence Iohannes Bramhton' Iohannes Letice Iohannes Sneterlee Adam Kent Iohannes Muriel Iohannes Scutteford Ricardus Steuenes et Iohannes de Wodhull' dicunt per sacramentum suum quod Robertus le Smyth' de Dunton' die Dominica in medio xlme anno regni regis Edwardi tercij tricesimo secundo apud Mulnho insultum fecit Willelmo Aylnoth' et ipsum verberauit et vulnerauit contra pacem. Item dicunt quod idem Robertus le Smyth' die Iouis proxima post festum purificacionis beate Marie anno regni regis Edwardi tercij tricesimo secundo apud Dunton' insultum fecit Ricardo Maggessone et ipsum verberauit et vulnerauit contra pacem. Qui quidem Robertus attachiatus fuit ad respondendum domino regi et fecit finem et dat domino regi viij s. per plegium Iohannis Tilbrok et Roberti Pagenho. (*Marg.* finem viij s.)

Robert le Smyth of Dunton, at Millow, assaulted William Aylnoth, beating and wounding him; at Dunton, he assaulted Richard Maggessone, beating and wounding him; being attached, he made a fine for 8s.; pledges, John Tilbrok, Robert Pagenho.

146. Robertus Holewelle[2] Robertus Tymcok Iohannes Buddenho Willelmus Freynshe Iohannes Freynshe Henricus Vmfrey Willelmus atteHo Iohannes Bateman Iohannes Boteler Iohannes Passewater Iohannes Fraunseys et Ricardus Englys dicunt per sacramentum suum quod Henricus Heyne de Coupol die Veneris proxima post festum decollacionis sancti Iohannis Baptiste anno regni regis Edwardi tercij tricesimo secundo apud Coupol insultum fecit Iohanni filio Iohannis Malyng seniori et ipsum verberauit vulnerauit et male tractauit contra pacem. Item dicunt quod idem Henricus attachiatus fuit per constabularios villate de Coupol per preceptum dictis constabularijs liberatum die Iouis proxima ante festum natiuitatis beate Marie anno supradicto apud Coupol et attachiamentum predictum vi et armis fregit. Qui quidem Henricus attachiatus fuit ad respondendum domino regi et fecit finem et dat domino regi x s. per plegium Simonis Maydelot et Iohannis Micche. (*Marg.* finem x s.)

Henry Heyne of Cople, at Cople, assaulted John son of John Malyng, sr., beating, wounding, and maltreating him; having been attached by the constables of the village and by order freed to them, he broke the attachment; being attached, he made a fine for 10s.; pledges, Simon Maydelot, John Micche.

147. Iohannes Holand[3] Thomas Spicer Hugo Lauche Willelmus Waryner Iohannes Frereman Willelmus Rauenesden Willelmus Rochewelle

---

[1] Jury 45.
[2] Jury 46.
[9] Jury 47.

Iohannes Sampson Iohannes Cook Thomas Vigerous Simon Warde et Radulfus Gy dicunt per sacramentum suum quod Iohannes Sadelere de Bedeford die Lune in crastino apostolorum Simonis et Iude anno regni regis Edwardi tercij tricesimo secundo apud Bed' in presencia iusticiariorum insultum fecit Rogero Mayn et cum cultello sanguinem ab eo extraxit contra pacem domini regis. Qui quidem Iohannes attachiatus fuit ad respondendum domino regi et fecit finem et dat domino regi xiij s. iiij d. per plegium Iohannis Frereman et Willelmi Rochewelle. (*Marg.* finem xiij s. iiij d.)

John Sadelere of Bedford, at Bedford, on 29 October 1358, in the presence of the justices assaulted Roger Mayn and with his knife drew blood; being attached, he made a fine for 13s. 4d.; pledges, John Frereman, William Rochewelle.

148. Dicunt eciam quod Iohannes le Shethere de Bed' fourbour die et anno supradictis apud Bed' insultum fecit eidem Rogero Mayn in presencia iusticiariorum cum gladio extracto contra pacem. Qui quidem Iohannes attachiatus fuit ad respondendum domino regi et fecit finem et dat domino regi xiij s. iiij d. per plegium Iohannis Frereman et Willelmi Rochewelle. (*Marg.* finem xiij s. iiij d.)

John le Shethere of Bedford weapon furbisher, at Bedford, on the same date, assaulted the same Roger Mayn in the presence of the justices with a drawn sword; being attached, he made a fine for 13s. 4d.; pledges, John Frereman, William Rochewelle.

149. Dicunt eciam quod Willelmus Bonseriaunt de Bed' die Sabati proxima post festum natiuitatis sancti Iohannis Baptiste anno regni regis Edwardi tercij tricesimo secundo apud Bed' noctanter insultum fecit Rogero Listere de Bed' et ipsum verberauit vulnerauit et male tractauit contra pacem cum ipse Rogerus custos fuit pacis domini regis. Qui quidem Willelmus attachiatus fuit ad respondendum domino regi et fecit finem et dat domino regi xiij s. iiij d. per plegium Willelmi Spicer et Iohannis of Alcherhalwen. (*Marg.* finem xiij s. iiij d.)

William Bonseriaunt of Bedford, at Bedford, at night assaulted Roger Listere of Bedford, beating, wounding, and maltreating him when Roger was custodian of the king's peace; being attached, he made a fine for 13s. 4d.; pledges, William Spicer, John of Alcherhalwen.

150. Henricus de Bereford[1] Robertus Lord Ricardus Englys Thomas Baa Thomas Saltere Walterus Voyse Iohannes Chanu Iohannes Golde de Diuelho Thomas Broun Simon Lache Iohannes le Beer et Euerardus Agu dicunt per sacramentum suum quod Petrus Aungeuyn de la Ford

[1]Jury 48.

die Sabati proxima post festum exaltacionis sancte crucis anno regni regis Edwardi tercij tricesimo secundo apud la Ford in Eton' insultum fecit Simoni Swafeld et eum verberauit vulnerauit et male tractauit contra pacem. Qui quidem Petrus attachiatus fuit ad respondendum domino regi et fecit finem et dat domino regi x s. per plegium Willelmi Sacomb senioris et Henricus Abbot. (*Marg.* finem x s.)

Peter Aungevyn of Eaton Ford, at Eaton Ford, assaulted Simon Swafeld, beating, wounding, and maltreating him; being attached, he made a fine for 10s.; pledges, William Sacomb, sr., Henry Abbot.

151. Dicunt eciam quod Robertus Terry de Bereford et Iohannes Sotul de Bereford die et festo omnium sanctorum anno regni regis Edwardi tercij tricesimo secundo apud Bereford insultum fecerunt Roberto Taillour et ipsum verberauerunt (et[1]) vulnerauerunt contra pacem. Qui quidem Robertus Terry et Iohannes attachiati fuerunt ad respondendum domino regi et dictus Robertus fecit finem et dat domino regi xl d. per plegium Thome Saltere et Walteri Voyse et dictus Iohannes fecit finem et dat domino regi ij s. per plegium predictum. (*Marg.* finem xl d. finem ij s.)

Robert Terry and John Sotul both of [Great] Barford, at Barford, assaulted Robert Taillour, beating and wounding him; being attached, they made fines, Robert for 40d., John for 2s.; pledges, Thomas Saltere, Walter Voyse.

152. Dicunt eciam quod Ricardus le Stockere de Begerye et Elizabeth' que fuit vxor Iohannis fitz Hugth' de Begerye die Martis in vigilia sancti Iacobi apostoli anno regni regis Edwardi tercij tricesimo secundo apud Begerye felonice interfecerunt Iohannem fitz Hugth' de Begerye et Petrum seruientem dicti Iohannis. Qui quidem Ricardus et Elizabeth' positi fuerunt in exigendis et per processum exacti de comitatu in comitatem quousque vtlagati fuerunt. (*Marg.* vtlagati)

Richard le Stockere and Elizabeth wife of John fitz Hugth both of Beggary, at Beggary, feloniously killed John fitz Hugth of Beggary and his servant Peter; they were exacted and outlawed.

153. Dicunt eciam quod Iohannes de Pertenhale de Chaluesterne insultum fecit Iohanni filio Iohannis et eum male verberauit cum baculo contra pacem. Qui quidem Iohannes de Pertenhale attachiatus fuit ad respondendum domino regi et fecit finem et dat domino regi v s. per plegium Willelmi Mordant iunioris et Willelmi Taillour. (*Marg.* finem v s.)

John de Pertenhale of Chawston assaulted John son of John and badly beat him with a stick; being attached, he made a fine for 5s.; pledges, William Mordant, jr., William Taillour.

154. Rogerus Bispham[1] Willelmus Oyldeboef' Iohannes Bolle Robertus Gardiner Willelmus Waukeleyn Robertus Trate Willelmus Masoun Willelmus Wysman Iohannes Cole turnour Iohannes le Eyr Iohannes Locusden' et Iohannes Molle dicunt per sacramentum suum quod Willelmus Barkere de Rislee Iohannes Tolous de Caysho Ricardus le Wrighte de Caysho et Iohannes Muleward de Caysho sunt communes malefactores et affrayatores pacis. Qui quidem Willelmus Iohannes Ricardus et Iohannes attachiati fuerunt ad respondendum domino regi et predictus Willelmus fecit finem et dat domino regi xl d. per plegium Iohannis Sayer et Thome Hutte et dictus Iohannes Tolous' fecit finem et dat domino regi ij s. per plegium Walteri le Eyr et Rogeri Dean et dictus Ricardus fecit finem et dat domino regi xviij d. per plegium Iohannis Parkere et Iohannis Goldyngton' et dictus Iohannes Muleward fecit finem et dat domino regi xl d. per plegium Willelmi atte Graunge et Willelmi Oyldeboef'. (*Marg.* finem xl d. finem ij s. finem xviij d. finem xl d.)

William Barkere of Riseley, John Tolous, Richard le Wrighte, and John Muleward all three of Keysoe, are common malefactors and affrayers; being attached, they all made fines ,William for 40d.; pledges, John Sayer, Thomas Hutte; John Tolous for 2s.; pledges, Walter le Eyr, Roger Dean; Richard for 18d.; pledges, John Parkere, John Goldyngton; John Muleward for 40d.; pledges, William atte Graunge, William Oyldeboef.

155. Iohannes le Whyte[2] Radulfus Litlee Ricardus Dauy Iohannes Dalton' Robertus Astel Thomas Hardy Willelmus oftheHul Robertus Auenel Iohannes Campyoun Thomas Frettere Iohannes Russel Thomas Bate et Ricardus Stockere dicunt per sacramentum suum quod Robertus Mariotessone le fysshere de Turueye die Mercurij proxima ante festum annunciacionis beate Marie anno regni regis Edwardi tercij tricesimo tercio apud Turueye insultum fecit Ade Wade de Turueye et eum verberauit et male tractauit contra pacem. Qui quidem Robertus attachiatus fuit ad respondendum domino regi et fecit finem et dat domino regi vj s. viij d. per plegium Iohannis de Ardres et Philippi le Fysshere. (*Marg.* finem vj s. viij d.)

Robert Mariotessone fisherman of Turvey, at Turvey, assaulted Adam Wade of Turvey, beating and maltreating him; being attached, he made a fine for 6s. 8d.; pledges, John de Ardres, Philip le Fysshere.

156. Dicunt eciam quod Ricardus Fourbour de Bed' die Dominica proxima post festum sancti Gregorij anno regni regis Edwardi tercij tricesimo tercio apud Bidenham insultum fecit Thome Colet de Bidenham et eum verberauit et vulnerauit contra pacem. Qui quidem Ricardus

[1]Jury 49.
[2]Jury 50.

7

attachiatus fuit ad respondendum domino regi et fecit finem et dat domino regi xl d. per plegium Roberti Waryner et Iohannis Boryate. (*Marg.* finem xl d.)

Richard Fourbour of Bedford, at Biddenham, assaulted Thomas Colet of Biddenham, beating and wounding him; being attached, he made a fine for 40d.; pledges, Robert Waryner, John Boryate.

157. Dicunt eciam quod Ricardus filius Stephani le Fullere de Bed' die et anno supradictis apud Bidenham intrauit clausum dicti Thome et sepes dicti Thome fregit et asportauit contra pacem. Qui quidem Ricardus attachiatus fuit ad respondendum domino regi et fecit finem et dat domino regi xviij d. per plegium Iohannis Blake et Willelmi Lauender. (*Marg.* finem xviij d.)

Richard son of Stephan le Fullere of Bedford, at Biddenham, entered the close of the aforesaid Thomas and broke and carried away his hedges; being attached, he made a fine for 40d.; pledges, John Blake, William Lavender.
[*m. 7*]

[*Endorsed*] Rotuli Reginaldi de Grey de Ruthyn et sociorum suorum (iusticiariorum[1]) custodendum pacis in comitatu Bed'

158. Henricus Abbot[1] Iohannes Baxtere Iohannes Bury Iohannes le Wrighte Iohannes Ropere Iohannes Cok Iohannes Golde de Diuelho Nicholaus Kepest iunior Iohannes Elys Walterus Auncel Iohannes Leychoft et Henricus Reignold dicunt per sacramentum suum quod Matillis Dolle die Dominica proxima ante festum sancti Valentini anno regni regis Edwardi tercij tricesimo tercio apud le Ford noctanter insultum fecit Agneti Pitosfrei et fregit caput suum contra pacem et Ricardus le Sawere de Iccombe venit in adiuuacionem dicte Matillis et percussit quemdam Willelmum Sacomb iuniorem contra pacem. Qui quidem Matillis et Ricardus attachiati fuerunt ad respondendum domino regi et dicta Matillis fecit finem et dat domino regi ij s. per plegium Roberti Dolle et Henrici Abbot et dictus Ricardus fecit finem et dat domino regi ij s. per plegium Iohannis Ropere et Iohannis Wrighte. (*Marg.* finem ij s. finem ij s.)

Matilda Dolle, at Eaton Ford, at night assaulted Agnes Pitosfrei and broke her head; Richard le Sawere of Incomb [Bucks] who aided Matilda hit William Sacomb, jr.; being attached, they each made a fine for 2s.; pledges, for Matilda, Robert Dolle, Henry Abbot; for Richard, John Ropere, John Wrighte.

[1]Jury 51.

159. Robertus Holewelle[1] Willelmus Clerk Willelmus Freynshe Iohannes atte March' Robertus Tymcok Willelmus Iuel Iohannes Burel Robertus Taillour Nicholaus Pecke Willelmus Craas Iohannes Buddenho et Iohannes Southe dicunt per sacramentum suum quod Nicholaus Taillour de Caldecote die Lune proxima post festum sancti Laurencij anno regni regis Edwardi tercij tricesimo secundo apud Caldecote cum alijs insultum fecit Iohanni atte Brook et eum verberauit vulnerauit et male tractauit contra pacem. Qui quidem Nicholaus attachiatus fuit ad respondendum domino regi et fecit finem et dat domino regi ij s. per plegium Iohannis Torold et Willelmi Freynshe. (*Marg.* finem ij s.)

Nicholas Taillour of Caldecote, at Caldecote, with others assaulted John atte Brook, beating, wounding, and maltreating him; being attached, he made a fine for 2s.; pledges, John Torold, William Freynshe.

160. Dicunt eciam quod Walterus Abel de Beuston' die Mercurij proxima ante festum exaltacionis sancte crucis anno regni regis Edwardi tercij tricesimo primo apud Bikeleswade vi et armis prosecutus est Iuonem atte Virok vsque ad portam Lincoln' in Bikeleswade et ibi insultum fecit ei verberando et minas occidendo contra pacem. Item dicunt quod idem Walterus die Veneris proxima ante festum ascensionis domini anno regni regis Edwardi tercij tricesimo tercio ad crucem in Ouerecaldecote predicto Iuoni vi et armis insultum fecit et minas occidendo et super hoc traxit cultellum suum vt eum occideret et ita fecisset nisi subsidium visinorum habuisset contra pacem. Qui quidem Walterus attachiatus fuit ad respondendum domino regi et fecit finem et dat domino regi xviij d. per plegium Willelmi Holecote et Iohannis Buddenho. (*Marg.* finem xviij d.)

Walter Abel of Beeston pursued Ivo atte Virok to the Lincoln gate in Biggleswade, assaulted him by beating, and threatened to kill him; at the cross in Upper Caldecote, he assaulted him, threatened him, and drawing his knife would have killed him but for the neighbours; being attached, he made a fine for 18d.; pledges, William Holecote, John Buddenho.

161. Dicunt eciam quod Simon Lucy et Iohannes Broun de Cherlton' in Mogerhanger die Iouis in tercia septimana proxima ante festum purificacionis beate Marie anno regni regis Edwardi tercij tricesimo secundo in quodam loco vocato le Laswe insultum fecerunt Willelmo atte Chambre vi et armis et eum verberauerunt et male tractauerunt contra pacem. Qui quidem Simon et Iohannes attachiati fuerunt ad respondendum domino regi et dictus Simon fecit finem et dat domino regi ij s. per plegium Iohannis Malyng et Iohannis de Buddenho et dictus Iohannes fecit finem et dat domino regi ij s. per plegium predictum. (*Marg.* finem ij s. finem ij s.)

[1]Jury 52.

Simon Lucy and John Broun of Chalton in Mogerhanger, in a place called Leasows, assaulted William atte Chambre, beating and maltreating him; being attached, they each made a fine for 2s.; pledges, John Malyng, John de Buddenho.

162. Willelmus Laurence[1] Iohannes de Wodhull' Thomas Nicol Iohannes Freynshe Thomas Child Iohannes Whyte Adam de Kent Iohannes de Bramhton' Iohannes Letice Robertus Pustel Willelmus Richeman et Iohannes Scotteford dicunt per sacramentum suum quod Willelmus Wethirherde de Saundeye die Lune circa festum sancti Barnabe anno regni regis Edwardi tercij tricesimo tercio apud Saundeye insultum fecit Iohanni de Oclee et ipsum verberauit et male tractauit contra pacem. Qui quidem Willelmus attachiatus fuit ad respondendum domino regi et fecit finem et dat domino regi xl d. per plegium Thome Child et Roberti Warde. (*Marg.* finem xl d.)

William Wethirherde of Sandy, at Sandy, assaulted John de Oclee, beating and maltreating him; being attached, he made a fine for 40d.; pledges, Thomas Child, Robert Warde.

163. Willelmus Bateman[2] Iohannes Saundres Iohannes Rolt Rogerus Deen Robertus Richard Walterus le Eyr Galfridus Torold Willelmus Godefrei Iohannes Raad Willelmus Warde Walterus Cartere et Barnabas Golde dicunt per sacramentum suum quod Ricardus Cristemasse et Agnes vxor eius die Veneris proxima post festum sancti Michelis anno regni regis Edwardi tercij tricesimo secundo apud Caysho intrauerunt clausum Henrici Daye contra pacem et dicta Agnes insultum fecit Eue vxori ipsius Henrici et eam verberauit contra pacem. Qui quidem Ricardus et Agnes attachiati fuerunt ad respondendum domino regi et fecerunt finem et dant domino regi v s. per plegium Willelmi atte Grange et Henrici filij Walteri. (*Marg.* finem v s.)

Richard Cristemasse and his wife Agnes, at Keysoe, entered the close of Henry Daye, where Agnes assaulted and beat Eva, Henry's wife; being attached, they made a fine for 5s.; pledges, William atte Grange, Henry son of Walter.

164. Dicunt eciam quod Iohannes Pozoun de Caysho die Dominica proxima post festum inuencionis sancte crucis anno regni regis Edwardi tercij tricesimo tercio apud Caysho clausum Henrici Daye intrauit et Euam vxorem dicti Henrici cepit et contra voluntatem suam eam stuperare voluerit contra pacem. Qui quidem Iohannes attachiatus fuit ad respondendum domino regi et fecit finem et dat domino regi ij s. per plegium predictum. (*Marg.* finem ij s.)

[1] Jury 53.
[2] Jury 54.

John Pozoun of Keysoe, at Keysoe, entered the close of Henry Daye, seized Henry's wife Eva to rape her; being attached, he made a fine for 2s.; pledges as above.

165. Dicunt eciam quod Iohannes Payn de Bolnhurst et Iohannes Benet de eadem die Martis proxima festum translacionis sancti Thome martiris anno regni regis Edwardi tercij tricesimo tercio apud Bolnhurst insultum fecerunt Emme vxori Petri ad Grangiam et eam verberauerunt et male tractauerunt cum vno baculo quousque iacuit super terram contra pacem et dictus Iohannes Benet est communis malefactor et affrayator pacis. Qui quidem Iohannes et Iohannes attachiati fuerunt ad respondendum domino regi et dictus Iohannes Payn fecit finem et dat domino regi xij d. per plegium Iohannis Astel et Willelmi atte Grange et dictus Iohannes Benet fecit finem et dat domino regi xij d. per plegium predictum. (*Marg.* finem xij d. finem xij d.)

John Payn and John Benet both of Bolnhurst, at Bolnhurst, assaulted Emma wife of Peter ad Grange, beating and maltreating her with a stick so that she lay on the ground; John Benet is a common malefactor and affrayor; being attached, they each made a fine for 12d.; pledges, John Astel, William atte Grange.

166. Iohannes le Rous[1] Gilbertus Colet Willelmus Botom Ricardus Wygeyn Iohannes Cartere de Goldyngton' Henricus Pippard Ricardus Brian Iohannes de Wodeford Galfridus Corner Ricardus Draper Ricardus Noble et Willelmus Stowe dicunt per sacramentum suum quod Willelmus Cartere de Bed' die Mercurij proxima ante festum decollacionis sancti Iohannis anno regni regis Edwardi tercij tricesimo tercio apud Puttenho iuxta Goldyngton' insultum fecit Willelmo Breustere de Bed' et eum verberauit vulnerauit et male tractauit contra pacem. Qui quidem Willelmus Cartere attachiatus fuit ad respondendum domino regi et fecit finem et dat domino regi v s. per plegium Iohannis Blake et Iohannis Cook'. (*Marg.* finem v s.)

William Cartere of Bedford, at Putnoe near Goldington, assaulted William Breustere of Bedford, beating, wounding, and maltreating him; being attached, he made a fine for 5s.; pledges, John Blake, John Cook.

167. Robertus Holewell'[2] Willelmus Clerk Willelmus Freynshe Iohannes atte March' Robertus Tymcok Willelmus Iuel Iohannes Burel Robertus Taillour Nicholaus Pecke Willelmus Craas Iohannes Buddenho et Iohannes Southe dicunt per sacramentum suum quod Willelmus Eyworthe de Bikeleswade die Lune in septimana pentecostes anno regni regis Edwardi tercij tricesimo tercio apud Bikeleswade insultum fecit Roberto

[1] Jury 55.
[2] Jury 56.

Buntyng de Bikeleswade et eum verberauit vulnerauit et mahemiauit contra pacem. Qui quidem Willelmus attachiatus fuit ad respondendum domino regi de transgressione predicta qui dicit quod dampnum quod fecit fuit in defensione sui corporis et aliter euadere non possit et de hoc ponit se super patriam. Ideo capiatur inde iurata que dicit quod dampnum quod fecit fuit in defensione sui corporis et aliter euadere non possit. Ideo eat inde quietus. (*Marg.* quietus)

William Eyworthe of Biggleswade, at Biggelswade, assaulted Robert Buntyng of Biggleswade, beating, wounding, and maltreating him; being attached, William pled self-defence and was acquitted.

168. Philipus Cawat[1] Nicholaus filius Roberti Willelmus Masoun Willelmus Waukeleyn Henricus filius Walteri Ricardus Staunford Iohannes Bolle Iohannes Saundres Walterus le Eyr Willelmus Oyldeboef de Pertenhale Stephanus de Holecote et Willelmus Permounter dicunt per sacramentum suum quod Radulfus le Webestere de Melcheborne capellanus die Iouis proxima ante festum apostolorum Petri et Pauli anno regni regis Edwardi tercij tricesimo tercio apud Melcheborne insultum fecit Iohanni Spenser et ipsum Iohannem maliciose vulnerauit cum vno cultello ita quod de vita sua desperabatur contra pacem. Qui quidem Radulfus attachiatus fuit ad respondendum domino regi et fecit finem et dat domino regi xiij s. iiij d. per plegium Iohannis Bolle et Willelmi Masoun. (*Marg.* finem xiij s. iiij d.)

Ralph le Webestere of Melchbourne chaplain, at Melchbourne, assaulted John Spenser and maliciously wounded him with a knife so that his life was endangered; being attached, he made a fine for 13s. 4d.; pledges, John Bolle, William Masoun.

169. Dicunt eciam quod Adam Tilneye de Melcheborne die Martis in septimana pentecostes anno regni regis Edwardi tercij triecsimo tercio apud Melcheborne cultellum suum tractauit Iohanni Spryngolf contra pacem et quod dictus Adam et Iohannes Tilneye de Melcheborne sunt communes affrayatores pacis. Qui quidem Adam et Iohannes attachiati fuerunt ad respondendum domino regi et dictus Adam fecit finem et dat domino regi xl d. per plegium Willelmi Masoun et Iohannis Molle et dictus Iohannes fecit finem et dat domino regi xl d. per plegium predictum. (*Marg.* finem xl d. finem xl d.)

Adam Tilneye of Melchbourne, at Melchbourne, drew his knife on John Spryngolf; he and John Tilneye of Melchbourne are common affrayers; being attached, they each made a fine for 40d.; pledges, William Masoun, John Molle.

[1]Jury 57.

170. Dicunt eciam quod Iohannes Spryngolf de Melcheborne die et anno supradictis attachiatus fuit per balliuum domini regis et per preceptum sibi liberatum et dictus Iohannes fregit attachiamentum balliui contra pacem. Qui quidem Iohannes attachiatus fuit ad respondendum domino regi et fecit finem et dat domino regi xl d. per plegium predictum. (*Marg.* finem xl d.)

John Spryngolf of Melchbourne being attached by the king's bailiff and released to himself, broke the attachment; being attached, he made a fine for 40d.; pledges as above.

171. Iohannes Cok¹ Willelmus Wyther Robertus Morle Gilbertus le Rous Willelmus Waryner Ricardus Bustlere Willelmus atte Halle Iohannes Bromham Henricus Harynger Iohannes Kerbrok Ricardus Cosse et Iohannes Welhul dicunt per sacramentum suum quod Willelmus Lilby de Clifton' et Henricus Braban de eadem die Veneris proxima ante festum translacionis sancti Thome anno regni regis Edwardi tercij tricesimo tercio apud Clifton' insultum fecerunt Roberto Dannessone et ipsum verberauerunt vulnerauerunt et male tractauerunt contra pacem. Qui quidem Willelmus et Henricus attachiati fuerunt ad respondendum domino regi et dictus Willelmus fecit finem et dat domino regi xl d. per plegium Rogeri atte Park et Iohannis Bullok et dictus Henricus fecit finem et dat domino regi xl d. per plegium predictum. (*Marg.* finem xl d. finem xl d.)

William Lilby and Henry Braban both of Clifton, at Clifton, assaulted Robert Dannessone, beating, wounding, and maltreating him; being attached, they each made a fine for 40d.; pledges, Roger atte Park, John Bullok.

[*m. 7d.*]
172. Willelmus de Kempston'² Thomas Peyntour Hugo Middulton' Henricus Arnold Hugo Lauche Willelmus Telloloue Henricus Sharman Willelmus Shirwode Iohannes Whyte Iohannes Daubour Radulfus Gy et Willelmus Crowe dicunt per sacramentum suum quod Willelmus le Rook die Mercurij proxima ante festum pasche anno regni regis nunc vicesimo octauo felonice furatus fuit vnam sellam equitaturam Iohannis le Waytte precij v s. apud Bed' et est communis malefactor. Qui quidem Willelmus captus fuit et in prisona detentus quousque deliberatus fuit coram Roberto de Thorp. (*Marg.* coram R de Thorp')

William le Rook feloniously stole a saddle, price 5s., from John le Waytte at Bedford; he is a common malefactor; he was freed from gaol before Robert de Thorp.

    See above no. 48.

¹Jury 58.
²Jury 59.

173. Dicunt eciam quod idem Willelmus anno regni regis nunc vicesimo sexto fecit se prouisorem domini regis sine warento capiendo aucas capones et galium de Katerina Boweles Iohanne le Taillour Matille de Kempston' et alijs et est communis malefactor et perturbator pacis quod quidem indictamentum missum fuit coram rege virtute quiusdam (breuis[1]) michi directi vt patet inferius in dicte breue. (*Marg.* coram rege)

The same William without a warrant made himself a purveyor of the king and took geese, capon, and cocks from Katherine Boweles, John le Taillour, Matilda de Kempston, and others; he is a common malefactor and disturber of the peace; this indictment was sent to the King's Bench by the writ below.

See above no. 48. Rook had previously been released to manucaptors on this offence; to be distrained for appearance before the King's Bench, Hilary 1358; in exigend in the King's Bench, Easter, Trinity, Michelmas, 1358; K.B. 390, Rex, m. 2; 391, Rex, m. 3d.; 392, Rex, m. 4; 393, Rex, m. 36d.

174. Dicunt eciam quod Isabella le Pipere et Margaria le Faucommer de Wolaston' anno regni regis nunc vicesimo octauo asportauerunt vnam ollam eream et patellam precij iij s. de Matille Astwode apud Bed' contra pacem et vnam clocam precij iiij s. de quodam extraneo apud Caldewelle contra pacem quod quidem indictamentum missum fuit coram rege virtute cuiusdam breuis michi directi vt patet inferius in dicto breui. (*Marg.* coram rege)

Isabelle le Pipere and Margery le Faucommer of Wyboston took a copper pot and plate, price 3s., from Matilda Astwode at Bedford and a cloak, price 4s., from a stranger at Cauldwell; this indictment was sent to the King's Bench by the writ below.

Both to be distrained for appearance before the King's Bench, Hilary 1358; in exigend in the King's Bench, Easter, Trinity, Michelmas 1358; K.B. 390, Rex, m. 2; 391, Rex, m. 3d.; 392, Rex, m. 4; 393, Rex, m. 36d.

175. Martinus le Eyr[1] Iohannes le Sweyn Ricardus Northwode Thomas Stepyngle Thomas Richer Iohannes atte Hokes Willelmus Conquest Iohannes de Marshton' Willelmus Doget Iohannes Lyllyngston Willelmus Richer et Robertus Deystere dicunt per sacramentum suum quod quidem extraneus dicens se vocari Ricardus de Oxenford simul cum Iohanne le Clerk bocher de Neuport et Iohanne Faucommer facientes se prouisores domini regis vbi non fuerunt et venerunt die Mercurij in crastino inuencionis sancte crucis anno regni regis Edwardi tercij tricesimo apud Wotton' et Kempston' et ceperunt de Thoma Drewe x oues et abduxerunt quousque dictus Thomas fecit finem cum predictis extraneo Iohanne et Iohanne de x s. et de Rogero Marchant eodem modo pro xx ouibus x s. et vnum annulum et de Thoma le Taillour et Iohanne Croude

[1] Jury 60.

eodem modo pro xviij ouibus vj s. viij d. et de Thoma Sternehull' eodem modo pro xiij ouibus iii s. iiij d. quod quidem indictamentum missum fuit coram rege virtute cuiusdem breuis michi directi vt patet inferius in dicto breui. (*Marg.* coram rege)

A stranger who called himself Richard de Oxenford with John le Clerk butcher of Newport [Bucks] and John Faucommer, all claiming to be royal purveyors, came to Wootton and Kempston and took ten sheep from Thomas Drewe forcing him to make a fine for 10s.; similarly from Roger Marchant twenty sheep for 10s. and a ring; from Thomas le Taillour and John Croude eighteen sheep for 6s. 8d.; from Thomas Sternehull thirteen sheep for 3s. 4d.; this indictment was sent to the King's Bench by the writ below.

All three to be distrained for appearance before the King's Bench, Hilary 1358; Oxenford and Faucommer in exigend in the King's Bench, Easter, Michelmas 1358; K.B. 390, Rex, m. 2; 391, Rex, m. 3d.; 392, Rex, m. 4; 393, Rex, m. 36d.; Clerk in exigend in the King's Bench, Easter, Trinity 1358; made a fine for 20s., Michelmas 1358; ibid., 391, Rex, m. 3d.; 392, Rex, m. 4; 393, Fines, m. 2d.

176. Iohannes de Kent[1] Adam de Kent Willelmus Mustel Iohannes de Wodhull' Thomas Nichol Iohannes de Bramhton' Iohannes Letice Willelmus Laurence Iohannes Freynshe Thomas Child Galfridus Haunuylle et Willelmus Richeman dicunt per sacramentum suum quod Athelina Flemyng die Mercurij proxima ante festum omnium sanctorum anno regni regis Edwardi tercij post conquestum tricesimo insultum fecit Isabelle vxori Iohannis Steke et eam verberauit et in fossata tractauit contra pacem quod quidem indictamentum missum fuit coram rege virtute cuiusdam breuis michi directi vt patet inferius. (*Marg.* coram rege)

Athelina Flemyng assaulted Isabelle wife of John Steke, beating her and dragging her in a ditch; this indictment was sent to the King's Bench by the writ below.

To be distrained for appearance before the King's Bench, Hilary 1358; in exigend in the King's Bench, Easter, Trinity, Michelmas 1358; made a fine for 40d., Michelmas 1358; K.B. 390, Rex, m. 2; 391, Rex, m. 3d.; 392, Rex, m. 4; 393, Rex, m. 36d.; ibid., Fines, m. 3.

177. Thomas Archer de Stepyngle[2] Reginaldus Iurdan Radulfus Clerk Thomas Sharpenho Ricardus Clerk Willelmus del Fermory Iohannes Northwode Willelmus Haukyn Iohannes le Lord Willelmus Wodeward Rogerus Blaunkfrount et Simon Loryng dicunt per sacramentum quod Iohannes Peyntour de Euersholt nuper manens in comitatu Bed' die

[1] Jury 61.
[2] Jury 62.

Dominica proxima post festum epiphanie anno regni regis nunc Anglie tricesimo felonice interfecit Simonem Wrawe de Euersholt et Henricum Tymmes de Euersholt. Item dicunt quod frater Willelmus de Langeleye prior ordinis fratrum predicatorum de Dunstapel receptauit eundem Iohannem Peyntour post feloniam factam sciens feloniam predictam. Et dicunt quod non receptus fuit alibi in comitatu Bed' nisi in eodem loco. Qui quidem Iohannes positus fuit in exigendis et per processum exactus de comitatu in comitatem quousque vtlagatus fuit. Et recordum et processum tangencia predictum fratrem Willelmum missa fuerunt coram rege virtute cuisdam breuis michi directi in hec verba. (*Marg.* vtlagatus coram rege)

John Peyntour of Eversholt formerly living in Bedfordshire feloniously killed Simon Wrawe and Henry Tymmes both of Eversholt; brother William de Langeleye, prior of Dunstable, received the said John knowing he had committed this felony; he was not received elsewhere in Bedfordshire; John was exacted and outlawed; the record on William was sent to the King's Bench by the writ below.

John Peyntour in exigend in the King's Bench, Hilary 1358; K.B. 390, Rex, m. 5; William de Langeleye in exigend in the King's Bench, Hilary 1358 and subsequently; pled not guilty and acquitted, Easter 1359, the principal having been outlawed; K.B. 390, Rex, m. 5d.; 391, Rex, m. 3d.; 392, Rex, m. 4; 393, Rex, m. 2d.; 395, Rex, m. 7d.

Edwardus dei gracia rex Anglie et Francie et dominus Hibernie dilectis et fidelibus suis Reginaldo de Grey et socijs suis iusticiarijs nostris ad pacem nostram in comitatu Bedeford conseruandam assignatis salutem. Quia quibusdam certis de causis cerciorari volumus super omnibus indictamentis coram vobis in comitatu predicto captis et penes vos residentibus inchoatis et nondum terminatis vobis mandamus quod indictamenta illa cum omnibus ea tangentibus mittatis coram nobis indilate vt vlterius inde fieri faciamus quod de iure et secundum legem et consuetudinem regni nostri Anglie inde fore viderimus faciendum et habeatis ibi hoc breue. Teste Willelmo de Notton' apud Dunstapele xij die Nouembris anno regni nostri Anglie tricesimo primo [1357] regni nostri Francie octauo.

Writ of cerciorari *to Grey and his associates ordering all undetermined indictments sent to the King's Bench. Issued by William de Notton at Dunstable, 12 November 1357.*

[*Endorsed*] Rotulus iusticiariorum custodium pacis et placita coram eis in comitatum Bedford tempore Edwardi tercij
Derby Edwardi tercij assise

SESSIONS OF THE PEACE,
1363-1364

ROLL B

Assize Roll 33

[m. 4]

Dominus Rex mandauit dilectis et fidelibus Thome de Reynes Willelmo de Risceby et Thome de Eston breue suum patens in hec verba. Edwardus dei gracia rex Anglie dominus Hibernie et Aquitanie dilectis et fidelibus suis Thome de Reynes Willelmo de Risceby et Thome de Eston salutem. Sciatis quod assignauimus vos coniunctim et diuisim ad pacem nostram et ad statuta apud Wynton' Norhamton' et Westm' pro conseruacione eiusdem pacis edita in comitatu Bedeford' tam infra libertates quam extra custodienda et custodiri facienda; et ad omnes illos quos contra formam statutorum predictorum delinquentes inueneritis castigandos et puniendos prout secundum formam statutorum predictorum fuerit faciendum; et ad omnes illos qui aliquibus de populo nostro de corporibus suis vel incendio domorum suarum minas fecerint per sufficientem securitatem de bono gestu suo erga nos et populum nostrum inueniendam compellandos et si huiusmodi securitatem facere recusauerint tunc eos in prisonis nostris quousque huiusmodi securitatem fecerint saluo custodiri faciendos. Assignauimus eciam vos vel duos vestrum iusticiarios nostros ad inquirendum per sacramentum proborum et legalium hominum de comitatu predicto tam infra libertates quam extra per quos rei veritas melius sciri poterit de quibuscumque felonijs et transgressionibus in comitatu predicto infra libertates et extra qualitercumque et per quoscumque factis et que extunc ibidem fieri contigerit et de receptatoribus manutentoribus et fautoribus malefactorum premissa perpetrantium ac alijs articulis et circumstancijs premissa qualitercumque contingentibus plenius veritatem; et eciam de hijs qui mensuris et ponderibus infra comitatum predictum infra libertates et extra contra formam statutorum et ordinacionum inde editorum iam vtuntur vel quos exnunc vti contigerit; et ad easdem felonias et transgressiones ad sectam nostram tantam et ad compota de collectoribus et receptoribus finium amerciamentorum et aliorum proficuorum de artificibus seruitoribus et alijs laboratoribus in comitatu predicto leuatorum et [leuandorum quos nuper communitati] regni nostri per termino trium annorum concessimus in auxilium decime [et quintedecime triennalium] quas eadem communitas nobis nuper concessit audienda et terminanda secundum legem et consuetudinem regni nostri; et ad dictos collectores et receptores compellendos [ad plenam] distribucionem de denarijs per ipsos inde collectis inter communitates villarum comitatus predicti [faciendam; necnon] ad debitam correccionem fieri faciendam de ponderibus et mensuris predictis [et condignam] punicionem illis quos de abusu ponderum et mensurarum predictorum culpabiles inueneritis [iuxta] formam ordinacionum et statutorum predictorum imponendam; eciam ad omnia indictamenta [coram] quibuscumque iusticiarijs nostris ad felonias et transgressiones in comitatu predicto temporibus preteritis audiendas et [terminandas assignatis facta et nondum] terminata inspicienda et ea debito fine terminanda secundum [legem et consuetudinem supradictas; et ad] omnes artifices seruitores et operarios quos contra formam [ordinacionum et] statutorum tam in parliamentis nostris ante hec tempora quam in presenti parliamento nostro [factorum delinquentes inueneritis] castigandos et puniendos prout secundum formam statutorum et ordinacionum [eorundem] fuerit faciendum. Et ideo vobis mandamus quod vos vel duo vestrum sessiones vestras quater [per annum super premissis] primo videlicet infra octabas epiphanie domini secundo infra secundam septimanam medie quadragesime tercio inter festa pentecostes et sancti Iohannis Baptiste et quarto infra octabas [sancti Michelis]; et ad certos dies et loca quos vos vel duo vestrum ad hoc prouideritis inquisiciones super [premissis faciatis]; et felonias transgressiones et compota predicta audiatis et terminetis et premissa omnia [et singula faciatis et] expleatis in forma predicta facturi inde quod ad iusticiam pertinet secundum legem et consuetudinem regni nostri saluis nobis amerciamentis et alijs ad nos inde spectantibus. Mandamus enim vicecomiti nostro comitatus predicti quod ad certos dies et loca quos vos vel duo vestrum ei scire faciatis venire faciat coram vobis vel duobus vestrum tot et tales probos et legales homines de balliua sua tam infra libertates quam extra per quos rei veritas in premissis melius sciri poterit et inquiri; et omnes articulos in ordinacionibus et statutis tam in parliamentis nostris ante hec tempora quam in presenti parliamento nostro factis et editis contentos conseruacionem dicte pacis nostre et punicionem artificium seruitorum et laboratorum concernentes vobis liberet exequendos. In cuius rei testimonium has litteras nostras fieri fecimus patentes. Teste me ipso apud Westm' xx die Nouembris anno regni nostri tricesimo sexto [1362].

Item dominus rex mandauit Reginaldo de Grey de Ruthyn et socijs suis nuper iusticiarijs ipsius domini regis ad diuersas felonias et transgressiones in eodem comitatu audiendas et terminandas assignatis ad mittendum coram prefatis Thoma et socijs suis hic omnia indictamenta ac recorda et processus coram eis incoata et non terminata quoddam breue domini regis clausum in hec verba.

Edwardus dei gracia rex Anglie dominus Hibernie et Aquitanie dilecto et fideli suo Reginaldo de Grey de Ruthyn salutem. Cum assignauimus dilectos et fideles nostros Thomam de Reynes Willelmum de Risceby et Thomam de Eston et duos eorum iusticiarios nostros ad diuersas felonias et transgressiones in comitatu Bed' audiendas et terminandas et ad omnia indictamenta de felonijs et transgressionibus in comitatu predicto coram vobis et socijs vestris nuper iusticiarijs nostris ad huiusmodi felonias et transgressiones in comitatu predicto audiendas et terminandas assignatis facta et nondum terminata inspicienda et debito fine terminanda secundum legem et consuetudinem regni nostri vobis mandamus quod ad certos dies et loca quos ijdem Thomas Willelmus et Thomas vel duo eorum vobis scire faciant indictamenta predicta ac processus inde nondum terminatos eisdem Thome Willelmo et Thome vel duobus eorum liberetis terminanda in forma predicta et habeatis ibi hoc breue. Teste me ipso apud Westm' xx die Nouembris anno regni nostri tricesimo sexto [1362].

Writ to Lord Grey instructing him to turn over any unfinished business to the newly appointed justices of the peace, Thomas de Reynes, William de Risceby, and Thomas de Eston.

Virtute cuius breuis idem Reginaldus misit iusticiarijs hic recordum et processus de quibus in dicto breui mencio in hec verba.

The following was sent.

1. (*Marg.* Bed') Iuratores comitatus Bed' videlicet Iohannes Estwyk Robertus Pustel Iohannes Frensh' Iohannes Clifton' Willelmus Stamford Willelmus Richeman Robertus Horle Robertus Warde Sampson Wright' Willelmus Rous Willelmus Frenssh' Willelmus Laurence et Iohannes atte Brok' alias coram Reginaldo de Grey et socijs suis nuper iusticiarijs ad diuersas felonias et transgressiones in comitatu Bed' audiendas et terminandas assignatis apud Bikeleswade presentauerunt quod die Dominica in vigilia assumpcionis beate Marie anno regni regis Edwardi tercij post conquestum tricesimo sexto apud Bikeleswade venerunt Iohannes filius Ricardi le Clerk de Stratton' Thomas filius Ricardi le Clerk de Stratton' Willelmus Dunton' de Bikeleswade et Willelmus Castel taillour vi et armis et Willelmum Child iuniorem et Thomam Child iuniorem verberauerunt et vulnerauerunt et predictum Willelmum Child iuniorem ibidem felonice interfecerunt. Per quod preceptum fuit vicecomiti quod caperet eos si etc.

At Biggleswade, John and Thomas sons of Richard le Clerk of Stratton, William Dunton of Bigglewsade, and William Castel tailor beat and wounded William Child, jr., and Thomas Child, jr., killing William; the sheriff is to arrest them.

See below no. 2.

[*m. 4d.*]

(*Marg.* Bed') Placita corone domini regis apud Bed' coram prefatis
Thoma de Reynes Willelmo de Risceby et Thoma de Eston' iusticiarijs
etc. die Martis proxima post festum sancti Gregorij anno regni regis
Edwardi tercij a conquestu tricesimo septimo [14 March 1363].

2. (*Marg.* Bed') Preceptum fuit vicecomiti quod caperet predictos
Iohannem filium Ricardi le Clerk Thomam filium Ricardi le Clerk
Willelmum Dunton' et Willelmum Castel si etc. et saluo etc. ita quod
haberet corpora eorum coram prefatis iusticiarijs vel duobus eorum ad
hunc diem etc. ad respondendum domino regi de felonijs et transgressionibus etc. Et modo scilicet ad predictum diem veniunt predicti Iohannes
Thomas et Willelmus Dunton' per vicecomitem ducti etc. et de predicto
Willelmo Castel vicecomes retornat quod ipse non est inuentus etc. Et
quia annus a tempore mortis ipsius Willelmi Child nondum elapsus est
et testatum est hic in curia quod Margareta que fuit vxor predicti Willelmi
Child prosequitur versus predictos Iohannem Thomam Willelmum
Dunton' Willelmum Castel ac quosdam alios de morte predicta per
appellum coram domino rege habitum etc. per quod ad deliberacionem
ipsorum Iohannis et aliorum legitime ad presens procedi non potest
quousque etc. Ideo ijdem Iohannes Thomas et Willelmus Dunton'
remittuntur prisone in custodia Petri de Salford' vicecomitis quousque
diem Mercurij proximum sequentem etc. Ad quem diem coram prefatis
Willelmo de Risceby et Thoma de Eston' apud Bed' veniunt predicti
Iohannes et alij per predictum vicecomitem ducti etc. et super hoc
dominus rex mandauit iusticiarijs hic quoddam recordum sub pede
sigilli sui in hec verba.

Edwardus dei gracia rex Anglie dominus Hibernie et Aquitanie dilectis
et fidelibus suis Thome de Reynes et socijs suis iusticiarijs ad diuersas
felonias et transgressiones in comitatu Bed' audicndas et terminandas
assignatis salutem. Transcriptum breuis de appello quod Margareta
que fuit vxor Willelmi Child de Bikeleswade iunioris in cancellaria
nostra de morte predicti Willelmi quondam viri sui versus Iohannem
filium Ricardi Clerk de Stratton' et alios in breui nostro predicto contentos impetrauit et coram nobis per vicecomitem Bed' fecit retornari
necnon certificacionem non prosecucionis ipsius Margarete appelli
predicti coram nobis facte vobis mittimus presentibus inclusum vt
securius ad deliberacionem ipsius Iohannis et aliorum in dicto breui
contentorum infra annum et diem a die mortis ipsius Willelmi procedere
poteritis prout de iure et secundum legem et consuetudinem regni nostri
fuerit faciendum. Teste me ipso apud Westm' xij die Februarij anno
regni nostri tricesimo septimo [1363].

Certificacio de quo in dicto breui fit mencio sequitur in hec verba.

Rex vult certis de causis cerciorari super tenore breuis de appello quod Margareta que fuit vxor Willelmi Child de Bikeleswade iunioris in cancellaria regis de morte predicti Willelmi quondam viri sui versus Iohannem filium Ricardi Clerk de Stratton' et alios in breui regio predicto contentos impetrauit et coram ipso rege per vicecomitem Bed' fecit retornari et si dictum breue ibidem fuerit prosecuta necne ideo transcriptum breuis predicti ac certificacio de ceteris premissis in cancellaria ipsius regis sub sigillo Henrici Grene capitalis iusticiarij sui distincte et aperte sine dilacione mittatur cum hac billa. Teste ipso rege apud Westm' x die Februarij anno regni sui tricesimo septimo [1363].

Transcriptum breuis de appello et similiter processus non prosecucionis de quo in dicto breui fit mencio et coram rege habiti sequitur in hec verba.

Edwardus dei gracia rex Anglie dominus Hibernie et Aquitanie vicecomiti Bed' salutem. Si Margareta que fuit vxor Willelmi Child de Bikeleswade iunioris fecerit te securum de clameo suo prosequendo tunc attachias Iohannem filium Ricardi Clerk de Stratton' Ricardum filium Ricardi Clerk de Stratton' Thomam filium Ricardi Clerk de Stratton' Stephanum Steuenes capellanum Iohannem Steuenes de Stratton' Iohannem Cook de Bikeleswade Iohannem Clerk de Bikeleswade et Matillem vxorem eius Willelmum Steuenes de Bikeleswade iuniorem Iohannem Raston' de Wrastlyngworth' Willelmum Laurence de Dunton' et Willelmum Castelman taillour per corpora sua secundum consuetudinem Anglie ita quod eos habeas coram nobis in octabis sancti Hillarij vbicumque tunc fuerimus in Anglia ad respondendum prefate Margarete de morte predicti Willelmi quondam viri sui vnde eos appellat et habeas ibi hoc breue. Teste me ipso apud Westm' xxv die Nouembris anno regni nostri tricesimo sexto [1362].

Ad quas octabas Hillarij coram domino rege apud Westm' veniunt predicti Iohannes Steuenes Iohannes Cook et Matillis per vicecomitem Bed' missi in proprijs personis suis. Et predicta Margareta licet quarto die placiti solempniter vocata non venit nec est prosecuta appellum suum ideo consideratum est quod plegij sui de prosecucione scilicet Thomas Child senior et Thomas Child iunior sint in misericordia et predicta Margareta capiatur set postea fecit finem cum domino rege occasione predicta vt patet in rotulo finium de termino sancti Hillarij predicto.

Et super hoc predicti Iohannes filius Ricardi Clerk Thomas filius Ricardi Clerk et Willelmus Dunton' instanter allocuti qualiter de felonia predicta se velint acquietare dicunt separatim quod isti in nullo sunt inde culpabilis et de bono et malo ponunt se super patriam ideo veniant inde iurata etc. Iuratores ad hoc electi triati et iurati dicunt super sacramentum suum quod ipsi in nullo sunt inde culpabiles nec vmquam se subtraxerunt occasione predicta. Ideo ipsi eant inde quieti et quo ad transgressionem predictam non possunt eam dedicere sed petunt se admitti ad finem faciendum cum domino rege occasione predicta et admittuntur prout patet in rotulo finium de ista sessione et eant inde sine die et quo ad prefatum Willelmum Castelman preceptum est vicecomiti quod capiat eum si etc. et saluo etc. ita quod habeat corpus eius coram prefatis iusticiarijs vel duobus eorum apud Bikeleswade die Iouis proxima [post clausum pasche] [13 April 1363] ad respondendum domino regi de quibusdam felonijs vnde indictatus est etc. (*Marg.* quieti)

The sheriff was ordered to arrest the aforesaid John and Thomas sons of Richard le Clerk, William Dunton, and William Castel. At an undated session he produced the first three but reported that Castel could not be found. Because a year had not elapsed since the death of Child and since his widow Margaret had lodged an appeal, the case could not proceed and the men were gaoled. In the King's Bench, Hilary 1363, Margaret failed to prosecute the appeal, her pledges were in mercy, and she made a fine. Because of the failure, Reynes and his associate justices of the peace for Bedfordshire were ordered to proceed with the trial of the offenders indicted before them by a writ of 12 February 1363 which is followed on the roll by a certification of the appeal, 10 February 1363, and a copy of the writ of appeal, 25 November 1362. At the session of the peace held at Bedford, 14 March 1363, three of the men appeared and, after a recital of the above facts, pled not guilty of the homicide, and were acquitted; they admitted the assault and made fines. William Castel did not appear and the sheriff is ordered to produce him at Biggleswade, 13 April 1363.

Record of the action was sent to chancery on a writ of 7 June 1364 and approval noted on 11 November 1364; Chancery Miscellany 47/5/125. For Margaret's fine of ½ mark in the King's Bench see K.B. 409, Fines, m. 1. For William Castel's failure to appear for trial and report of his outlawry see below nos. 13, 34.

Plus de sessione isto in rotulo sequente

[*m. 3*]
(*Marg.* Bed') Placita corone coram prefatis Thoma de Reynes Willelmo de Risceby et Thoma de Eston iusticiarijs etc. die Martis proximo post festum sancti Gregorij anno regni regis Edwardi tercij tricesimo septimo predicto [14 March 1363].

Rex mandauit Reginaldo de Grey de Ruthyn et socijs suis nuper iusticiarijs etc. ad mittendum coram prefatis Thoma et socijs suis hic omnia indictamenta ac recorda et processus coram eis incoata et non terminata quodam breue domini regis clausum in hec verba.

Edwardus dei gracia rex Anglie dominus Hibernie et Aquitanie dilecto et fideli suo Reginaldo de Grey de Ruthyn salutem. Cum assignauimus dilectos et fideles nostros Thomam de Reynes Willelmum de Risceby et

Thomam de Eston et duos eorum iusticiarios nostros ad diuersas felonias et transgressiones in comitatu Bed' audiendas et terminandas et ad omnia indictamenta de felonijs et transgressionibus in comitatu predicto coram vobis et socijs vestris nuper iusticiarijs nostris ad huiusmodi felonias et transgressiones in comitatu predicto audiendas et terminandas assignatis facta et non dum terminata inspicienda et debito fine terminanda secundum legem et consuetudinem regni nostri vobis mandamus quos (ad[1]) certos dies et loca quos ijdem Thomas Willelmus et Thomas vel duo eorum vobis scire faciant indictamenta predicta ac processus inde nondum terminatos eisdem Thome Willelmo et Thome vel duobus eorum liberatis terminanda in forma predicta et habeatis ibi hic breue. Teste me ipso apud Westm' xx die Nouembris anno regni nostri tricesimo sexto [1362].

A repetition of the writ on p. 101.

Virtute cuius breuis idem Reginaldus misit iusticiarijs hic recordum et processus de quo in dicto breui mencio in hec verba.

The following was sent.

3. (*Marg.* Bed') Iohannes Beweles de magna Holewelle captus pro eo quod ipse die Veneris proxima ante festum sancte Margarete virginis anno regni regis Edwardi tercij a conquestu tricesimo sexto apud Shefford Thomam de la Dale de Piryton se defendendo interfecit vnde coram Iohanne de Meperteshale[1] Thoma de Eston et Willelmo de Otford[1] iusticiarijs ad pacem domini regis etc. indictatus est et modo venit per vicecomitem ductus et allocutus est qualiter se velit de felonia predicta acquietare dicit quod ipse in nullo est inde culpabilis et de bono et malo ponit se super patriam. Iuratores ad hoc electi et iurati dicunt super sacramentum suum quod die et anno predictis quedam contencio inter predictum Iohannem Beweles et predictum Thomam de la Dale ex malicia et insultu ipsius Thome apud Shefford ad domum Willelmi Wycher oriebatur ita quod idem Thomas extraxit gladium suum et ipsum Iohannen prosecutus fuit in domum predictam ad ipsum interficiendum et ipsum Iohannem fugauit ad quamdam parietem in eadem domo qui quidem Iohannes percipiens mortem sibi iminere et se nullo modo absque mortis periculo vlterius posset diffugere extraxit gladium suum precij vj d. et ipsum Thomam de la Dale in pectore percussit vsque ad cor vnde statim obijt iuratores quesiti si idem Iohannes aliquo modo viuus euasisse potuisset dicunt precise quod non et dicunt quod idem Iohannes non ex aliqua felonia seu malicia precogitata set se ipsum defendendo ipsum Thomam interfecit etc. Ideo idem Iohannes

---

[1] Associated with the Bedfordshire peace commission of 21 March 1361; *C.P.R.,* 1361–1364, pp. 8, 66, 67.

8

committitur prisone ad graciam domini regis expectandam etc. Et super hoc venerunt Iohannes Creueker Iohannes Dageneye et alij et manuceperunt pro predicto Iohanne Beweles habendum corpus eius coram prefatis iusticiarijs ad proximam sessionem etc. et sic etc. quousque etc. Qua die Martis supradicto coram prefatis Thoma de Reynes Willelmo de Risceby et Thoma de Eston iusticiarijs etc. idem Iohannes Beweles venit hic et dicit quod dominus rex pardonauit eidem Iohanni sectam pacis sue etc. per litteras suas patentes quas profert in hec verba.

Edwardus dei gracia rex Anglie dominus Hibernie et Aquitanie omnibus balliuis et fidelibus suis ad quos presentes littere peruenerint salutem. Quia accepimus per recordum dilectorum et fidelium nostrorum Iohannis de Mepersale et sociorum suorum nuper iusticiariorum nostrorum ad diuersas felonias et transgressiones et alia malefacta in comitatu Bed' tam infra libertates quam extra audiendas et terminandas assignatorum quod Iohannes Beweles de magna Holewell captus et detentus in gaola nostra Bed' pro morte Thome de la Dale de Piryton vnde rectatus est interfecit ipsum Thomam se defendendo ita quod mortem propriam aliter euadere non potuit et non per feloniam aut maliciam excogitatem nos pietate moti pardonauimus eidem Iohanni sectam pacis nostre que ad nos pertinet pro morte predicta et firmam pacem nostram ei inde concedimus ita tamen quod stet recto in curia nostra si quis versus eum loqui voluerit de morte predicta. In cuius rei testimonium has litteras nostras fieri fecimus patentes. Teste me ipso apud Westm' x die Februarij anno regni nostri tricesimo septimo [1363].

Virtute quarum litterarum idem Iohannes Beweles eat inde quietus et super hoc veniunt Iohannes Creueker Iohannes Dagenay Willelmus Freynsh et Galfridus Creueker et manucapiunt pro predicto Iohanne de bono gestu suo et de pace etc. erga dominum regem et populum suum etc. (*Marg.* quietus manucaptores)

John Beweles of Holwell [Herts] was indicted for killing Thomas de la Dale of Pirton [Herts] in self-defence; he pleads not guilty; the jury says that contention arose between the said John and the said Thomas in the house of William Wycher at Shefford, whereupon Thomas drew his sword, pursued John into the house so that John was forced to kill Thomas to save his own life. John produces a pardon which is given in full, and is acquitted.

4. (*Marg.* Bed') Iuratores comitatus Bed' presentant quod Willelmus Okele de Launden et Willelmus filius Simonis le Chapman anno regni regis nunc xxxvij^{mo} apud Turueye quemdam Iohannem Orkebold attachiatum per constabularios de Turueye a posessione eorum abstraxerunt et eum a comitatu Bed' in comitatu Buk' conduxerunt contra statutum etc. Per quod preceptum est vicecomiti quod capiat eos si etc. et eos saluo etc. ita quod habeat corpora eorum coram prefatis iusticiarijs vel

duobus eorum apud Bikeleswade die Iouis proxima post clausum pasche [13 April 1363] ad respondendum domino regi de premissis etc.

William Okele of Lavendon [Bucks] and William son of Simon le Chapman, at Turvey, dragged John Orkebold from the constables of Turvey who had arrested him to send him into Buckinghamshire. The sheriff is to produce them before the justices at Biggleswade, 13 April 1363.

For fine made by William Okele see below no. 18; for subsequent summons of William son of Simon le Chapman and report of outlawry see below nos. 18, 21, 30, 43.

5. Item presentant quod Ricardus Drynkewel et Willelmus Wyse die Lune proxima post festum sancti Valentini anno regni regis Edwardi tercij tricesimo septimo veniebant cum gladijs et arcubus in Carlton contra pacem et maliciose prosequebantur Ricardum Bailly in manerio de Carltonehalle eum ad interficiendum etc. Item dicunt quod Iohannes Campioun de Carlton erat bercarius et reiuit illud officium et modo est tegulator contra statutum etc. Per quod preceptum est vicecomiti quod capiat predictos Ricardum Willelmum et Iohannem si etc. et eos saluo etc. ita quod habeat corpora eorum coram prefatis iusticiarijs vel duobus eorum apud Bikeleswade die Iouis proxima post clausum pasche [13 April 1363] ad respondendum domino regi de premissis etc. (*Marg.* capiat)

Richard Drynkewel and William Wyse being armed, at Carlton, pursued Richard Bailly to the manor of Carlton Hall to kill him. John Campioun who was a shepherd has become a slater contrary to the Statute [of Labourers]. The sheriff is ordered to produce the three men for trial at Biggleswade, 13 April 1363.

For fine made by Richard Drynkewel see below no. 18; for subsequent summons and report of outlawry of the other two see below nos. 18, 21, 30, 43.

6. (*Marg.* Bed') Iuratores comitatus Bed' presentant quod Adam Irrysheman Iohannes Welsheman et Laurencius Welsheman de Wotton capiunt lucrum excessiuum contra statutum pro bladis triturandis videlicet pro quolibet quarterio frumenti iij d. ob. et quarterio omniscumque generis bladorum iij d. etc. Per quod preceptum est vicecomiti quod capiat eos si etc. et saluo etc. ita quod habeat corpora eorum coram prefatis iusticiarijs vel duobus eorum apud Bikeleswade die Martis proxima post octabas trinitatis [6 June 1363] ad respondendum domino regi de premissis etc. (*Marg.* capiat)

Adam Irrysheman, John Welsheman, and Laurence Welsheman of Wootton took excess wages for sowing grain, i.e., for each quarter of corn, 3d., ob., of other grains, 3d. The sheriff is to produce the three men for trial before the justices at Biggleswade, 6 June 1363.

For summons and report of outlawry see below nos. 21, 31, 43.

7. (*Marg.* Bed') Iuratores comitatus Bed' presentant quod Iohannes seruiens Agnetis Garkyn de Northeuele Robertus Thacchere de Stanford et Adam seruiens Iohannis Hertebourne ceperunt in artificijs suis excessiuum lucrum contra statutum etc. Per quod preceptum est vicecomiti quod capiat eos si etc. et eos saluo etc. ita quod habeat corpora eorum coram prefatis iusticiarijs apud Bed' die Iouis in septimana pentecostes [25 May 1363] ad respondendum domino regi de premissis etc. (*Marg.* capiat)

John servant of Agnes Garkyn of Northill, Robert Thacchere of Stanford, and Adam servant of John Hertebourne took excessive wages; the sheriff is to produce them for trial before the justices at Bedford, 25 May 1363.

For summons and report of outlawry see below nos. 21, 26, 41.

[*m. 3d.*]
(*Marg.* Bed') Placita coram prefatis Willelmo et Thoma de Eston iusticiarijs die Iouis proxima post festum sancti Gregorij anno tricesimo septimo supradicto [16 March 1363].

8. (*Marg.* Bed') Iuratores villate de Bed' presentant quod Thomas Pichard qui vtlagatus est pro felonia (receptus est[1]) ad domum Isabelle vxoris eius contra pacem et voluntatem hominum villate Bed'. Per quod preceptum est vicecomiti quod capiat eos si etc. et eos saluo etc. ita quod habeat corpora eorum coram prefatis iusticiarijs apud Bed' die Iouis in septimana pentecostes tunc proxima sequente [25 May 1363] ad respondendum domino regi super premisses etc. (*Marg.* capiat)

Thomas Pichard outlawed for felony was received by his wife Isabel against the wishes of the townsmen; the sheriff is to produce both of them for trial before the justices at Bedford, 25 May 1363.

For summons for both see below no. 19; for report of outlawry for Thomas and of illness for Isabel see below no. 44.

9. Willelmus Iuel captus est pro eo quod ipse die Mercurij in festo sancte crucis anno regni regis Edwardi tercij tricesimo sexto apud Beuston insultum fecit Iohanni Pysel et brachium sinistrum? fregit et male tractauit contra pacem etc. et pro eo quod ipse die Iouis proxima ante festum sancti Iohannis Baptiste anno regni regis Edwardi tercij tricesimo quinto apud Beuston insultum fecit Willelmo Cartere et ipsum verberauit contra pacem etc. vnde indictatus est. Et modo venit per vicecomitem ductus et cognoscit transgressiones predictas et petit se admitti ad finem faciendum cum domino rege occasionibus predictis et admittitur prout patet per rotulum finium de ista sessione. Ideo eat inde sine die etc. (*Marg.* finem)

William Ivel appears because he has been indicted for assaulting John Pysel and breaking his left arm, and assaulting and beating William Cartere;

both were done at Beeston. He admits to these trespasses, makes a fine, and is sine die.

10. Hugo Cole et Iohannes Mordon capti sunt pro eo quod die Mercurij in festo sancte crucis anno regni regis Edwardi tercij tricesimo sexto apud Beuston simul pugnauerunt et quilibet eorum verberauit alterum contra pacem etc. vnde indictati sunt. Et modo veniunt per vicecomitem ducti et petunt se admitti ad finem faciendum cum domino rege occasione predicta et admittuntur prout patet per rotulum finium etc. (*Marg.* fines)

Hugh Cole and John Mordon appear because they had been indicted for fighting and wounding each other; they each make a fine.

11. Iuratores comitatus Bed' presentant quod Iohannes filius Iohannis de Euesham die Iouis proxima ante festum sancti Petri aduincula anno regni regis Edwardi tercij xxxvj^{to} apud Ampthull insultum fecit cuidam homini domini principis et ipsum verberauit vulnerauit et male tractauit contra pacem. Et dicunt quod Hugo Caus fuit coadiutor illius transgressionis etc. Per quod preceptum est vicecomiti quod capiat eos si etc. et eos saluo etc. ita quod habeat corpora eorum coram prefatis iusticiarijs apud Bed' die Iouis in septimana pentecostes [25 May 1363] ad respondendum domino regi de premissis etc. (*Marg.* capiat)

John son of John de Evesham, at Ampthill, assaulted a certain man of the chief lord, beating, wounding, and maltreating him; Hugh Caus joined him in committing this trespass. The sheriff is to produce them for trial before the justices at Bedford, 25 May 1363.

For fine made by Hugh Caus see below no. 20; for summons and sheriff's failure to produce John son of John see below nos. 20, 40.

12. Item presentant quod Iohannes Sedekyn filius Nigelli Daye de Mershton die Iouis proxima ante festum sancti Petri aduincula anno regni regis Edwardi tercij tricesimo sexto apud Crannfeld felonice furatus fuit duos equos precij viij s. de Simone Bale per quod captus fuit et (in^{i}) prisona detentus quousque ductus fuit per vicecomitem coram Roberto de Thorp et socijs suis iusticiarijs etc. apud Dunstapul etc.

John Sedekyn son of Nigel Daye of Marston, at Cranfield, feloniously stole two horses, price 8s., from Simon Bale; being in prison he was tried before Robert de Thorp at Dunstable.

John son of Nigel atte Hurne of Marston was tried before Robert de Thorpe and John Knyvet delivering Dunstable gaol, 23 February 1364, for two thefts of horses at Woburn Chapel; he was judged guilty and sentenced to be hanged; G.D.R. 223/1, m. 110. I am indebted to Mr. C. A. F. Meekings for calling my attention to this gaol delivery file.

Placita coram prefatis iusticiarijs apud Bikeleswade die Iouis proxima post clausum pasche anno tricesimo septimo supradicto [13 April 1363].

13. (*Marg.* Bed') Preceptum fuit vicecomiti quod caperet Willelmum Castel taillour si etc. et saluo etc. ita quod haberet corpus eius hic ad hunc diem ad respondendum domino regi de quibusdam felonijs vnde indictatus est et vicecomes retornat quod ipse non est inuentus etc. Ideo preceptum est vicecomiti quod exigi faceret eum de comitatu in comitatum quousque etc. si non etc. et si etc. tunc eum capiat et saluo etc. ita quod habeat corpus eius coram prefatis iusticiarijs apud Bed' die Lune proxima post festum sancti Michelis [2 October 1363] ad respondendum domino regi de premissis etc. (*Marg.* capiat)

William Castel tailour whom the sheriff was to produce to answer for felonies for which he has been indicted, does not appear; the sheriff is to have him exacted and to produce him before the justices for trial at Bedford, 2 October 1363.
See above nos. 1, 2; for report of outlawry see below no. 34.

14. Nicholaus Croule fullere Iohannes Curteys de Turueye et Walterus seruiens dicti Iohannis capti sunt pro eo quod die Mercurij in vigilia ascencionis domini anno regni regis Edwardi tercij tricesimo quinto apud Bed' insultum fecerunt Iohanni Lageby et ipsum verberauerunt vulnerauerunt et male tractauerunt contra pacem etc. vnde indictati sunt. Et modo veniunt per vicecomitem ducti et petunt se admitti ad finem faciendum cum domino rege occasione predicta et admittuntur prout per rotulum finium etc. (*Marg.* fines)

Nicholas Croule fuller, John Curteys of Turvey, and his servant Walter appear because they have been indicted for assaulting, beating, wounding, and maltreating John Lageby, at Bedford; they each make a fine.

15. Iuratores comitatus Bed' presentant quod Robertus Irrysh quondam seruiens Willelmi Mordant de Stepynglee die Mercurij proxima post festum sancti Michelis anno regni regis Edwardi tercij xxxv^{to} apud Stepynglee felonice furatus fuit sex arietes precij vj s. de Thoma Stepynglee etc.

Robert Irrysh former servant of William Mordant of Steppingley, at Steppingley, feloniously stole six ewes, price 6s., from Thomas Stepynglee.
See below no. 17.

16. Item presentant quod Iohannes Stacy de Wotton Pelyng receptauit de die in diem et de nocte in noctem Thomam Pichard et alios ignotis qui vtlagati sunt pro felonijs etc.

John Stacy of Wootton Pillinge daily and nightly received Thomas Pichard and others unknown who were outlawed for felony.
See below no. 17.

17. Item presentant quod Walterus Swon de Barkshyre die Iouis proxima post festum omnium sanctorum anno regni regis Edwardi tercij xxxv^to apud Wottonpelyng domum Petri Hare felonice fregit et j quarterium frumenti et j quarterium pisarum precij vj s. felonice furatus fuit de dicto Petro item quod idem Walterus die et anno supradictis apud Wottonepelyng felonice furatus fuit vj s. in pecunia numerata de Gaueto Cartere etc. Per quod preceptum est vicecomiti quod capiat predictos Robertum Iohannem et Walterum si etc. et saluo etc. ita quod habeat corpora eorum coram prefatis iusticiarijs apud Bed' die Iouis in septimana pentecostes [25 May 1363] ad respondendum domino regi de premissis etc. (*Marg.* capiat)

Walter Swon of Berkshire, at Wootton Pillinge, felonioulsy broke into the house of Peter Hare and stole one quarter of corn and one quarter of peas, price 6s.; he feloniously stole 6s. in cash from Gavet Cartere. The sheriff is to produce Robert [Irrysh], John [Stacy], and Walter [Swon] before the justices for trial at Bedford, 25 May 1363.

See above nos. 15, 16; for subsequent summons and report of outlawry for all three see below nos. 22, 44.

18. (*Marg.* Bed') Preceptum fuit vicecomiti quod caperet Willelmum Okelee de Laundon Willelmum filium Simonis le Chapman Ricardum Drynkewel Willelmum Wyse et Iohannem Campioun de Carlton si etc. et saluo etc. ita quod haberet corpora eorum hic ad hunc diem ad respondendum domino regi de diuersis transgressionibus oppresionibus grauaminibus et excessibus vnde indictati sunt. Et predicti Willelmus Okelee et Ricardus Drynkewel venerunt per vicecomitem ducti et petunt admitti ad finem faciendum cum domino rege occasionibus predictis et admittuntur prout patet per rotulum finium etc. et quo ad predictos Willelmum filium Simonis Chapman Willelmum Wyse et Iohannem Campioun vicecomes retornat quod non sunt inuenti etc. Ideo preceptum est vicecomiti sicut alia quod eos capiat etc. et eos saluo etc. ita quod habeat corpora eorum coram prefatis iusticiarijs etc. apud Bikeleswade die Martis proxima post octabas sancte trinitatis [6 June 1363] ad respondendum domino regi etc. (*Marg.* capiat)

The sheriff has been ordered to produce William Okelee of Lavendon [Bucks], William son of Simon le Chapman, Richard Drynkewel, William Wyse, and John Campioun of Carlton who have been indicted for trespass. Okelee and Drynkewel appear and make fines; the sheriff is to produce the others for trial before the justices at Biggleswade, 6 June 1363.

For the indictments see above nos. 4, 5; for subsequent summons for William son of Simon, William Wyse, and John Campioun see below nos. 21, 30, 43.

[*m. 2*]

(*Marg.* Bed') Placita coram Willelmo de Rysceby et Thoma de Eston iusticiarijs domini regis etc. apud Bed' die Iouis in septimana pentecostes anno tricesimo septimo supradicto [25 May 1363].

19. (*Marg.* Bed') Preceptum fuit vicecomiti quod caperet Thomam Pychard (et Isabellam vxorem eius[i]) etc. et saluo etc. ita quod haberet corpora eorum coram prefatis iusticiarijs hic ad hunc diem ad respondendum domino regi de diuersis felonijs vnde indictati sunt et vicecomes retornat quod ipsi non sunt inuenti etc. Ideo preceptum est vicecomiti quod exigi faciat eos de comitatu in comitatum quousque etc. si non etc. et si etc. tunc eos capiat etc. et saluo etc. ita quod habeat corpora eorum coram prefatis iusticiarijs apud Bed' die Lune proxima post festum epiphanie domini [8 January 1364] ad respondendum domino regi de premissis etc.

The sheriff does not produce Thomas Pychard and his wife Isabel who were indicted for felony; they are to be exacted and the sheriff is to produce them for trial before the justices at Bedford, 8 January 1364.

For the indictment of Isabel see above no. 8; for report of Thomas' outlawry and Isabel's illness in prison see below no. 44.

20. (*Marg.* Bed') Preceptum fuit vicecomiti sicut pluries quod caperet Iohannem filium Iohannis Euesham et Hugonem Caus si etc. et saluo etc. ita quos haberet corpora eorum coram prefatis iusticiarijs hic ad hunc diem ad respondendum domino regi de diuersis transgressionibus contra pacem factis vnde indictati sunt. Et modo venit predictus Hugo per vicecomitem ductus et petit se admitti ad finem faciendum cum domino rege occasione predicta et admittitur prout patet per rotulum finium etc. et quo ad predictum Iohannem vicecomes retornat quod ipse non est inuentus etc. Ideo preceptum est vicecomiti quod exigi faciat eum de comitatu in comitatum quousque etc. si non etc. et si etc. tunc eum capiat etc. et saluo etc, ita quod habeat corpus eius coram prefatis iusticiarijs apud Bed' die Lune proxima post festum epiphanie domini [8 January 1364] ad respondendum domino regi de premissis etc.

The sheriff has been ordered to produce John son of John Evesham and Hugh Caus who were indicted for trespass; Hugh appears and makes a fine; John is to be exacted and the sheriff is to produce him for trial before the justices at Bedford, 8 January 1364.

For the indictments see above no. 11; for the sheriff's failure to produce John see below no. 40.

21. (*Marg.* Bed') Preceptum fuit vicecomiti sicut pluries quod caperet

Willelmum filium Simonis le Chapman Iohannem Campion de Carlton
Willelmum Wyse Adam Irryssheman Iohannem Welsheman Laurencium
Welsheman de Wotton Iohannem seruientum Agnetis Garkyn de Nort-
gouele Robertum Thecchere de Stanford et Adam seruientem Iohannis
Hertebourne si etc. et saluo etc. ita quod haberet corpora eorum coram
prefatis iusticiarijs hic ad hunc diem ad respondendum domino regi de
diuersis transgressionibus oppresionibus grauaminibus et excessibus
vnde indictati sunt. Et vicecomes retornat quod ipsi non (sunt[1]) inuenti
etc. Ideo preceptum est vicecomiti quod exigi faciat eos de comitatu in
comitatum quousque etc. si non etc. et si etc. tunc eos capiat etc. et
saluo etc. ita quod habeat corpora eorum coram prefatis iusticiarijs apud
Bed' die Lune proxima post festum epiphanie domini [8 January 1364]
ad respondendum domino regi de premissis etc.

The sheriff has been ordered to produce William son of Simon le Chapman,
John Campion of Carlton, William Wyse, Adam Irryssheman, John
Welsheman, Laurence Welsheman of Wootton, John servant of Agnes
Garkyn of Northill, Robert Thecchere of Stanford, and Adam servant of
John Hertebourne who were indicted for trespass; as they fail to appear
they are to be exacted and the sheriff is to produce them for trial before the
justices at Bedford, 8 January 1364.
    For the indictments see above nos. 4, 5, 6, 7; for non-appearance by
William son of Simon, William Wyse, and John Campion see above no. 18;
for subsequent summons and report of outlawry for all nine see below nos.
26, 30, 31, 41, 43.

22. (*Marg.* Bed') Preceptum fuit vicecomiti quod caperet Robertum
Irrysh quondam seruientem Willelmi Mordant de Stepynglee Iohannem
Stacy de Wotton Pelyng et Walterum Swon de Barkshyre si etc. et saluo
etc. ita quod haberet corpora eorum coram prefatis iusticiarijs hic ad hunc
diem ad respondendum domino regi de diuersis felonijs vnde in dictati sunt.
Et vicecomes retornat quod ipsi non sunt inuenti etc. Ideo preceptum
est vicecomiti quod exigi faciat eos de comitatu in comitatum quousque
etc. si non etc. et si etc. tunc eos capiat etc. et saluo etc. ita quod habeat
corpora eorum coram prefatis iusticiarijs apud Bed' die Lune proxima
post festum epiphanie domini [8 January 1364] ad respondendum domino
regi de premissis etc.

The sheriff has been ordered to produce Robert Irrysh former servant of
William Mordant of Steppingley, John Stacy of Wootton Pillinge, and
Walter Swon of Berkshire who were indicted for felony; as they fail to
appear they are to be exacted and the sheriff is to produce them for trial
before the justices at Bedford, 8 January 1364.
    For the indictments see above nos. 15, 16, 17; for report of outlawry see
below no. 44.

23. Iohannes Hayle de Bolnhurst senior captus est pro eo quod die Dominica proxima post festum decollacionis sancti [Iohannis Baptiste] anno regni regis Edwardi tercij tricesimo sexto apud Bolnhurst insultum fecit Waltero Cartere de Bolnhurst et Augustino de Stoghton et ipsos verberauit vulnerauit et male tractauit contra pacem etc. vnde indictatus est. Et modo venit per vicecomitem ductus et petit se admitti ad finem faciendum cum domino rege occasione predicta et admittitur prout patet per rotulum finium etc. (*Marg.* finem)

John Hayle of Bolnhurst, sr., who was indicted for assaulting, beating, wounding, and maltreating Walter Cartere of Bolnhurst and Augustine de Stoghton, at Bolnhurst, appears and makes a fine.

24. Iohannes Coppelowe de Bolnhurst et Walterus Bere of Bolnhurst capti sunt pro eo quod die Dominica proxima post festum sancti Matthie apostoli anno regni regis Edwardi tercij tricesimo septimo apud Pertenhale insultum fecerunt Galfrido Soutere et ipsum verberauerunt vulnerauerunt et male tractauerunt contra pacem etc. vnde indictati sunt. Et modo veniunt per vicecomitem ducti et petunt se admitti ad finem faciendum cum domino rege occasione predicta et admittuntur prout patet per rotulum finium etc. (*Marg.* fines)

John Coppelowe and Walter Bere both of Bolnhurst who were indicted for assaulting, beating, wounding, and maltreating Geoffrey Soutere, at Pertenhall, appear and make fines.

25. Adm vicarius ecclesie de Oclee captus est pro eo quod die Lune proxima ante festum sancti Nicholai anno regni regis Edwardi tercij tricesimo quinto apud Oclee insultum fecit Ade Polat et ipsum prosecutus fuit cum vno cultello tracto vsque ad ecclesiam de Oclee et ibidem ipsum verberauit et male tractauit contra pacem etc. vnde indictatus est. Et modo venit per vicecomitem ductus et petit se admitti ad finem faciendum cum domino rege occasione predicta et admittitur prout patet per rotulum finium etc. (*Marg.* finem)

Adam vicar of Oakley who was indicted for assaulting Adam Polet and pursuing him with a drawn knife to the church at Oakley, appears and makes a fine.

26. (*Marg.* Bed') Preceptum fuit vicecomiti quod caperet Iohannem seruientem Agnetis Garkyn de Northzouele Robertum Thecchere de Stannford et Adam seruientem Iohannis Hertebourne si etc. et saluo etc. ita quod haberet corpora eorum coram prefatis iusticiarijs hic ad hunc diem ad respondendum domino regi de diuersis transgressionibus oppresionibus et excessibus vnde indictati sunt Et vicecomes modo retornat quod ipsi non sunt inuenti etc. Ideo preceptum est vicecomiti

quod exigi faciat eos de comitatu in comitatum quousque etc. si non etc. et si etc. tunc eos capiat et saluo etc. ita quod habeat corpora eorum coram prefatis iusticiarijs apud Bed' die Lune proxima post festum epiphanie domini [8 January 1364] ad respondendum domino regi de premissis etc.

The sheriff was ordered to produce John servant of Agnes Garkyn of North-hill, Robert Thecchere of Stanford, and Adam servant of John Hertebourne who were indicted for trespass; as they fail to appear they are to be exacted and the sheriff is to produce them for trial before the justices at Bedford, 8 January 1364.

For the indictments see above no. 7; for previous failure to appear see above no. 21; for outlawry see below no. 41.

[*m. 2d.*]
Placita coram prefatis iusticiarijs apud Bikeleswade die Martis proxima post octabas trinitatis anno tricesimo septimo supradicto [6 June 1363].

27. (*Marg.* Bed') Ricardus Waryn' de Sondeye Walterus Waryn' de Sondeye Robertus le Smyth' de Sondeye Iohannes Becke Iohannes Bethewater de Sondeye et Willelmus Rochewell capti sunt pro eo quod die Lune proxima post festum sancti Gregorij pape anno regni regis Edwardi tercij post conquestum tricesimo septimo venerunt ad pontem de Bykeleswade in hundredo de Wixt' vi et armis ex malicia precogitata et ibidem Thome de Adyngraue insultum fecerunt et ipsum verberauerunt vulnerauerunt mahemiauerunt et male tractauerunt contra pacem etc. vnde indictati sunt. Et modo veniunt per vicecomitem ducti et petunt se admitti ad finem faciendum cum domino rege occasione predicta et admittuntur prout patet per rotulum finium etc. (*Marg.* fines)

Richard Waryn of Sandy, Walter Waryn of Sandy, Robert le Smyth of Sandy, John Becke, John Bethewater of Sandy, and William Rochewell, who were indicted for assaulting, beating, wounding, maltreating, and committing mayhem with malice aforethought on Thomas de Adyngrave at the bridge from Biggleswade, appear and make fines.

28. (*Marg.* Bed') Willelmus Taillour de Euerton Henricus Gerneys et Iohannes Attewell de Euerton capti sunt pro eo quod die Dominica proxima post festum sancti Hillarij anno regni regis Edwardi tercij post conquestum tricesimo sexto venerunt apud Temesford et ibidem vi et armis insultum fecerunt Willelmo Lambard et ipsum verberauerunt vulnerauerunt et male tractauerunt contra pacem vnde indictati sunt. Et modo veniunt per vicecomitem ducti et petunt se admitti ad finem

faciendum cum domino rege occasione predicta et admittuntur prout patet per rotulum finium etc. (*Marg.* fines)

William Taillour of Everton, Henry Gerneys, and John Attewell of Everton who were indicted for assaulting, beating, wounding, and maltreating William Lambard, at Tempsford, appear and make fines.

29. (*Marg.* Bed') Iuratores comitatus Bed' presentant quod Robertus Loty capellanus die Dominica proxima post festum sancte trinitatis anno regni regis Edwardi tercij a conquestu tricesimo septimo apud le brigge de Blounham obuiauit Roberto Strote de Blounham ex ira precogitata et ibidem predictus Robertus Loty insultum fecit eidem Roberto Strote et ibidem dictus Robertus Strote in sua defensione dictum Robertum Loty capellanum interfecit cum vno baculo precij j d. per quod preceptum est vicecomiti quod caperet predictum Robertum Strote si etc. et (eum¹) saluo etc. ita quod habeat corpus eius coram prefatis iusticiarijs apud Shefford die Sabati proxima post quindenam sancti Iohannis [15 July 1363] ad respondendum domino regi de premissis etc (*Marg.* capiat)

Robert Loty chaplain, at the bridge at Blunham, waylaid Robert Strote of Blunham maliciously and assaulted him; in self-defence Robert Strote killed Robert Loty with a stick, price 1d.; the sheriff is to produce Strote for trial before the justices at Shefford, 15 July 1363.
    For subsequent summons and report of outlawry see below nos. 32, 42.

30. (*Marg.* Bed') Preceptum fuit vicecomiti sicut pluries quod caperet Willelmum filium Simonis le Chapman Willelmum Wyse et Iohannem Campioun de Carlton si etc. et saluo etc. ita quod haberet corpora eorum hic ad hunc diem ad respondendum domino regi etc. Et vicecomes retornat quod non sunt inuenti etc. Ideo preceptum est vicecomiti quod exigi faciat eos de comitatu in comitatum quousque etc. si non etc. et si etc. tunc eos capiat et saluo etc. ita quod habeat corpora eorum coram prefatis iusticiarijs apud Bed' die Lune proxima post festum epiphanie domini [8 January 1364] ad respondendum domino regi etc. (*Marg.* capiat)
The sheriff was ordered to produce William son of Simon le Chapman, William Wyse, and John Campioun of Carlton; as they fail to appear they are to be exacted and the sheriff is to produce them for trial before the justices at Bedford, 8 January 1364.
    For indictments see above nos. 4, 5; for previous failure to appear see above nos. 18, 21; for report of outlawry see below no. 43.

31. (*Marg.* Bed') Preceptum fuit vicecomiti sicut pluries quod caperet Adam Irrysheman Iohannem Welsheman et Laurencium Walshman de Wotton si etc. et saluo etc. ita quod haberet corpora eorum hic ad hunc

diem ad respondendum domino regi etc. Et vicecomes retornat quod non sunt inuenti etc. Ideo preceptum est vicecomiti quod exigi faciat eos de comitatu in comitatum quousque etc. si non etc. et si etc. tunc eos capiat et saluo etc. ita quod habeat corpora eorum coram prefatis iusticiarijs apud Bed' die Lune proxima post festum epiphanie domini [8 January 1364] ad respondendum domino regi etc. (*Marg.* capiat)

The sheriff was ordered to produce Adam Irrysheman, John Welsheman, and Laurence Walshman; as they fail to appear they are to be exacted and the sheriff is to produce them for trial before the justices at Bedford, 8 January 1364.

For indictments see above no. 6; for previous failure to appear see above no. 21; for report of outlawry see below no. 43.

Placita coram prefatis iusticiarijs apud Shefford die Sabati proxima post quindenam sancti Iohannis anno tricesimo septimo supradicto [15 July 1363].

32. (*Marg.* Bed') Preceptum fuit vicecomiti quod caperet Robertum Strote de Blounham si etc. et saluo etc. ita quod haberet corpus eius hic ad hunc diem ad respondendum domino regi de quibusque felonijs vnde indictatus est. Et vicecomes retornat quod ipse non est inuentus etc. Ideo preceptum est vicecomiti quod exigi faciat eum de comitatu in comitatum quousque etc. si non etc. et si etc. tunc eum capiat et saluo etc. ita quod habeat corpus eius coram prefatis iusticiarijs apud Bed' die Lune proxima post festum epiphanie domini [8 January 1364] ad respondendum domino regi de premissis etc. (*Marg.* capiat)

The sheriff was ordered to produce Robert Strote of Blunham who had been indicted for felony; as he fails to appear, he is to be exacted and the sheriff is to produce him for trial before the justices at Bedford, 8 January 1364.

For the indictment see above no. 29; for report of outlawry see below no. 42.

33. Robertus Warde tannere de Bikeleswade et Thomas Child senior tannere de Bikeleswade capti sunt pro eo quod presentatum est super ipsos quod ipsi vendiderunt corea tannata in foro de Shefford et ceperunt lucrum excessiuum videlicet in quilibet xij d. iiij d. contra statutum. Et modo veniunt per vicecomitem ducti coram prefatis iusticiarijs hic et allocuti sunt qualiter se velint de premisses acquietare dicunt quod ipsi in nullo sunt inde culpabiles contra statutum et de bono et malo ponunt se super patriam. Iuratores ad hoc electi et iurati dicunt super sacramentum suum quod in nullo sunt inde culpabiles. Ideo ipsi eant inde quieti sine die etc. (*Marg.* quieti)

Robert Warde and Thomas Child, sr., tanners of Biggleswade, are pro-

duced because it was presented that they had sold tanned hides in the market at Shefford, charging an extra 4d. in the shilling, against the Statute [of Labourers]; they plead not guilty and the jury acquits them.

[*Endorsed upside down in a different hand*] Placita corone in comitatu Bed' anno 37° Edwardi tertij

[*m. 1d.*]
Placita coram prefatis Willelmo de Risceby et Thoma de Eston iusticiarijs apud Bed' die Lune proxima post festum sancti Michelis anno regni regis Edwardi tercij tricesimo septimo supradicto [2 October 1363].

34. (*Marg.* Bed') Preceptum fuit vicecomiti quod exigi faceret Willelmum Castel taillour de comitatu in comitatum quousque etc. si non etc. et si etc. tunc eum caperet et saluo etc. ita quod haberet corpus eius coram prefatis iusticiarijs hic ad hunc diem ad respondendum domino regi de diuersis felonijs vnde indictatus est. Et vicecomes modo retornat quod ad comitatum Bed' tentum ibidem die Lune proxima ante festum pentecostes anno regni regis Edwardi tercij a conquestu tricesimo septimo predictus Willelmus Castel taillour primo exactus fuit et non comparuit et sic de comitatu in comitatum quousque ad comitatum Bed' tentum ibidem die Lune proxima ante festum natiuitatis beate Marie virginis anno supradicto predictus Willelmus Castel taillour quinto exactus fuit et non comparuit. Ideo ad iudicium per Iohannem Child et Iohannis [*sic*] Pertesoyl coronatores comitatus predicti vtlagatus est per quod inquiratur de terris et catallis suis etc. (*Marg.* vtlagatus inquiratur)

The sheriff was ordered to have William Castel tailor exacted and produce him to answer for the felony for which he was indicted; the sheriff reports that Castel, having been exacted at five county courts between May and September 1363, has been outlawed before the coroners, John Child and John Pertesoyl.

For the indictment and previous summons see above nos. 1, 2, 13.

35. (*Marg.* Bed') Preceptum fuit vicecomiti quod exigi faceret Rogerum Drynkewel de comitatu in comitatum quousque etc. si non etc. et si etc. tunc eum caperet et saluo etc. ita quod haberet corpus eius coram prefatis iusticiarijs hic ad hunc diem ad respondendum Ricardo balliuo de Carlton halle de placito contemptus et transgressionis qui tam pro domino rege quam pro se ipso versus eum per billam prosequitur. Et vicecomes modo retornat quod ad comitatum Bed' tentum ibidem die Lune proxima ante festum sancti Georgij anno regni regis Edwardi tercij a conquestu tricesimo septimo Rogerus Drynkewel primo exactus fuit et non comparuit et sic de comitatu in comitatum quousque ad comitatum Bed' tentum ibidem die Lune proxima ante festum natiuitatis beate Marie virginis anno supradicto predictus Rogerus Drynkewel

quinto exactus fuit et non comparuit. Ideo ad iudicium per Iohannem
Child et Iohannem Pertesoyl coronatores comitatus predicti vtlagatus
est per quod inquiratur de terris et catallis suis etc. (*Marg.* vtlagatus
inquiratur)

*The sheriff was ordered to have Roger Drynkewel exacted and produce him
to answer to Richard bailiff of Carlton Hall in a plea of contempt and
trespass; the sheriff reports that Drynkewel, having been exacted in five
county courts between April and September 1363, has been outlawed
before the coroners, John Child and John Pertesoyl.*

36. (*Marg.* Bed') Radulfus Berde de Wilde captus est pro eo quod die
Dominica proxima ante festum purificacionis beate Marie virginis anno
regni regis Edwardi tercij tricesimo septimo apud Wilden insultum fecit
Iohanni Hamond et ipsum verberauit vulnerauit et male tractauit contra
pacem. Et modo venit per vicecomitem ductus et petit se admitti ad
finem faciendum cum domino rege occasione predicta et admittitur
prout patet per rotulum finium etc.

*Ralph Berde of Wilden is produced because, at Wilden, he assaulted John
Hamond, beating, wounding, and maltreating him; he makes a fine.*

37. (*Marg.* Bed') Henricus Bretoun de Shefford captus est pro eo quod
ipse die Lune proxima post festum sancti Petri in cathedra anno regni
regis Edwardi tercij a conquestu tricesimo septimo apud Shefford felonice
furatus fuit duo linthiamina precij xj d. et quod dictus Henricus arettattus
est de male fama latrocinij vnde indictatus est. Et modo venit per
vicecomitem ductus et allocutus est qualiter se velit de premisses acquietare dicit quod in nullo est inde culpabilis et de bono et malo ponit
se super patriam. Iuratores ad hoc electi et iurati qui dicunt super sacramentum suum quod predictus Henricus in nullo est inde culpabilis nec
se retraxit occasione predicta. Ideo eat inde quietus etc. (*Marg.* quietus)

*Henry Bretoun who was indicted for feloniously stealing two sheets, price
11d., at Shefford and because he had been arrested for ill repute as a thief,
appears and pleads not guilty; the jury acquits him.*

38. (*Marg.* Bed') Nicholaus Hayward de Faldo captus pro eo quod ipse
die Iouis in festo sancte Katerine virginis anno regni regis Edwardi
tercij a conquestu tricesimo quinto apud Strattele felonice depredauit
Iohannem Valeys de xl s. argenti et est communis latro vnde indictatus
est. Et modo venit per vicecomitem ductus et allocutus est qualiter se
velit de felonia predicta acquietare dicit quod in nullo est inde culpabilis
et de bono et malo ponit se super patriam. Iuratores ad hoc electi et
iurati qui dicunt super sacramentum suum quod predictus Nicholaus in

nullo est inde culapbilis nec se vmquam retraxit occasione predicta. Ideo eat inde quietus etc. (*Marg.* quietus)

Nicholas Hayward of Faldo who was indicted because, at Streatley, he feloniously robbed John Valeys of 40s. and as a common thief, pleads not guilty and is acquitted.

39. (*Marg.* Bed') Willelmus Sacomb senior Henricus Abbot et Iohannes de Bury capti sunt pro eo quod ipsi ceperunt in artificijs suis vendendo corea tannata excessiuum lucrum videlicet in xij d. iiij [?] d. contra statutum etc. vnde indictati sunt etc. Et modo veniunt per vicecomitem ducti et allocuti sunt qualiter se velint de premissis acquietare et dicunt quod ipsi nuper coram Reginaldo de Grey et socijs suis nuper iusticiarijs in comitatu predicto etc. pro quibusdam excessibus coram eisdem iusticiarijs tunc presentatis fecerunt finem et dicunt quod a tempore finis predicte facte vsque ad diem presentacionis nunc facte non ceperunt lucrum excessiuum prout super ipsos presentatum est et de hoc ponunt se super patriam. Iuratores ad hoc electi et iurati qui dicunt super sacramentum suum quod a tempore finis facte ad diem presentacionis predicte in nullo sunt inde culpabiles. Ideo eant inde quieti etc. (*Marg.* quieti)

William Sacomb, sr., Henry Abbot, and John de Bury, produced because they are indicted for selling tanned hides at 4d. extra in the shilling, say that they have already made fines before Reginald de Grey and his associates, former justices of the peace, and that since that time they have not charged excess prices; they are acquitted.

[*m. 1*]
Placita coram Willelmo de Risceby et Thoma de Eston' iusticiarijs regis etc. apud Bed' die Lune proxima post festum epiphanie domini anno regni regis Edwardi tercij a conquestu tricesimo septimo [8 January 1364].

40. (*Marg.* Bed') Preceptum fuit vicecomiti quod exigi faceret Iohannem filium Iohannis de Euesham et Robertum Bron seruientem Iohannis de Aylesbury militis de comitatu in comitatem quousque etc. si non etc. et si etc. tunc eos caperet et saluo etc. ita quod haberet corpora eorum coram prefatis iusticiarijs hic ad hunc diem ad respondendum domino regi de diuersis transgressionibus et opprecionibus vnde indictati sunt. Et vicecomes modo retornat quod eos cepit quos non habet hic ad hunc diem. Ideo vicecomes in misericordia domini regis prout patet per rotulum finium et amerciamentorum.

The sheriff was ordered to have John son of John de Evesham and Robert Bron servant of John de Aylesbury, Kt., exacted and to produce

them to answer for the trespasses for which they were indicted; because the
sheriff, who had them in charge, no longer has them he is amerced.

For the indictment and failure to appear of John son of John see above
nos. 11, 20; no indictment of Robert Bron appears on this roll.

41. (*Marg.* Bed') Preceptum fuit vicecomiti quod exigi faceret Iohannem
seruientem Agnetis Garkyn de Northzeuele Robertum Thechere de
Stanforde et Adam seruientem Iohannis Hertebourne de comitatu in
comitatum quousque etc. si non etc. et si etc. tunc eos caperet et saluo
etc. ita quod haberet corpora eorum coram prefatis iusticiarijs hic ad
hunc diem ad respondendum domino regi de diuersis contemptibus
extorsionibus et excessibus vnde indictati sunt. Et vicecomes modo
retornat quod ad comitatum Bed' tentum ibidem die Lune proxima post
festum translacionis sancti Thome martiris anno regni regis Edwardi
tercij a conquestu tricesimo septimo predicti Iohannes Robertus et Adam
primo exacti fuerunt et non comparuerunt et sic de comitatu in comitatum
quousque ad comitatum Bed' tentum ibidem die Lune proxima ante
festum omnium sanctorum anno supradicto predicti Iohannes seruiens
Agnetis Garkyn Robertus Thechere et Adam seruiens Iohannis Hertebourne quinto exacti fuerunt et non comparuerunt. Ideo ad iudicium
per Iohannem Child et Iohannem Pertesoyl coronatores comitatus
predicti vtlagati sunt per quod inquiratur de terris et catallis suis etc.
(*Marg.* vtlagati inquiratur)

The sheriff was ordered to have John servant of Agnes Garkyn of Northill,
Robert Thechere of Stanford, and Adam servant of John Hertebourne
exacted and to produce them to answer for the trespasses for which they
were indicted; the sheriff reports that having been exacted in five county
courts between July and October 1363 they have been outlawed before the
coroners, John Child and John Pertesoyl.

For the indictments and previous failure to appear see above nos. 7, 21,
26.

42. (*Marg.* Bed') Preceptum fuit vicecomiti quod exigi faceret Robertum
Strote de Blounham de comitatu in comitatum quousque etc. si non etc.
et si etc. tunc eum caperet et saluo etc. ita quod haberet corpus eius
coram prefatis iusticiarijs hic ad hunc diem ad respondendum domino
regi de diuersis felonijs vnde indictatus est. Et vicecomes modo retornat
quod ad comitatum Bed' tentum ibidem die Lune proxima ante festum
natiuitatis beate Marie virginis anno regni regis Edwardi tercij a conquestu tricesimo septimo predictus Robertus primo exactus fuit et non
comparuit et sic de comitatu in comitatum quousque ad comitatum Bed'
tentum ibidem die Lune in festo natalis domini anno supradicto predictus
Robertus quinto exactus fuit et non comparuit. Ideo ad iudicium per
Iohannem Child et Iohannem Pertesoyl coronatores comitatus predicti

9

vtlagatus est per quod inquiratur de terris et catallis suis etc. (*Marg.* vtlagatus inquiratur)

The sheriff was ordered to have Robert Strote of Blunham exacted and to produce him to answer for the felonies for which he was indicted; the sheriff reports that having been exacted in five county courts between September and December 1363, he has been outlawed before the coroners, John Child and John Pertesoyl.

For the indictment and previous failure to appear see above nos. 29, 32.

43. (*Marg.* Bed') Preceptum fuit vicecomiti quod exigi faceret Willelmum filium Simonis le Chapman Willelmum Wyse Iohannem Campioun de Carlton Adam Irryshman Iohannem Welsheman et Laurencium Welsheman de Wotton de comitatu in comitatum quousque etc. si non etc. et si etc. tunc eos caperet et saluo etc. ita quod haberet corpora eorum coram prefatis iusticiarijs hic ad hunc diem ad respondendum domino regi de diuersis transgressionibus oppressionibus extorsionibus et excessibus vnde indictati sunt. Et vicecomes modo retornat quod ad comitatum Bed' tentum ibidem die Lune proxima post festum translacionis sancti Thome martiris anno regni regis Edwardi tercij a conquestu tricesimo septimo predicti Willelmus filius Simonis le Chapman et alij in breue nominati primo exacti fuerunt et non comparuerunt et sic de comitatu in comitatum quousque ad comitatum Bed' tentum ibidem die Lune proxima ante festum omnium sanctorum anno supradicto predicti Willelmus filius Simonis et omnes alij quinto exacti fuerunt et non comparuerunt. Ideo ad iudicium per Iohannem Child et Iohannem Pertesoyl coronatores comitatus predicti vtlagati sunt per quod inquiratur de terris et catallis etc. (*Marg.* vtlagati inquiratur)

The sheriff was ordered to have William son of Simon le Chapman, William Wyse, John Campioun of Carlton, Adam Irryshman, John Welsheman, and Laurence Welsheman exacted and to produce them to answer for the trespasses for which they were indicted; the sheriff reports that having been exacted in five county courts between July and October 1363, they have been outlawed before the coroners, John Child and John Pertesoyl.

For the indictments see above nos. 4, 5, 6; for previous summons see above nos. 18, 21, 30, 31.

44. (*Marg.* Bed') Preceptum fuit vicecomiti quod exigi faceret Robertum Irrysch quondam seruientem Willelmi Mordant de Stepynglee Iohannem Stacy de Wotton' Pelyng Walterum Swon de Barkshyre Thomam Pychard et Isabellam vxorem eius de comitatu in comitatum quousque etc. si non etc. et si etc. tunc eos caperet et saluo etc. ita quod haberet corpora eorum coram prefatis iusticiarijs hic ad hunc diem ad respondendum domino regi de diuersis felonijs vnde indictati sunt. Et vicecomes modo

retornat quod ad comitatum Bed' tentum ibidem die Lune proxima post festum translacionis sancti Thome martiris anno regni regis Edwardi tercij a conquestu tricesimo septimo predicti Robertus Irrysch et alij in breue nominati primo exacti fuerunt et non comparuerunt et sic de comitatu in comitatum quousque ad comitatum Bed' tentum ibidem die Lune proxima ante festum omnium sanctorum anno supradicto predicti Robertus Irrysch et omnes alij quinto exacti fuerunt et predicta Isabella comparuit et eam in prisona domini regis tanta infirmitata detenta est quod eam hic ad hunc diem ducere non potuit et predicti Robertus Irrysch Iohannes Stacy Walterus Swon et Thomas Pychard non comparuerunt. Ideo ad iudicium per Iohannem Child et Iohannem Pertesoyl coronatores comitatus predicti vtlagati sunt per quod inquiratur de terris et catallis suis etc. (*Marg.* vtlagati inquiratur)

The sheriff was ordered to have Robert Irrysch former servant of William Mordant of Steppingley, John Stacy of Wootton Pillinge, Walter Swon of Berkshire, Thomas and Isabel Pychard exacted and to produce them to answer for the felonies for which they are indicted; the sheriff reports that Isabel is ill in prison and cannot appear and that the men, having been exacted in five county courts between July and October 1363 were outlawed before the coroners, John Child and John Pertesoyl.

For the indictments see above nos. 8, 15, 16, 17; for previous failure to appear see above nos. 19, 22.

9*

INDEX OF PERSONS AND PLACES

The numbers in brackets refer to the numbers of the cases on the peace rolls. Place names have been indexed under their modern forms, with a cross reference from the form in the text. Places in counties other than Bedford have been so identified.

Abbreviations: s.—son; w.—wife; wid.—widow.

INDEX OF SUBJECTS

Except for official and occupational designations and references to the Statute of Labourers material in the cases has not been indexed.